THE WORK OF
TEACHING WRITING

THE WORK OF TEACHING WRITING

Learning from Fiction, Film, and Drama

JOSEPH HARRIS

UTAH STATE UNIVERSITY PRESS
Logan

© 2020 by University Press of Colorado

Published by Utah State University Press
An imprint of University Press of Colorado
245 Century Circle, Suite 202
Louisville, Colorado 80027

ASSOCIATION of UNIVERSITY PRESSES   The University Press of Colorado is a proud member of the Association of University Presses.

The University Press of Colorado is a cooperative publishing enterprise supported, in part, by Adams State University, Colorado State University, Fort Lewis College, Metropolitan State University of Denver, Regis University, University of Colorado, University of Northern Colorado, University of Wyoming, Utah State University, and Western Colorado University.

∞ This paper meets the requirements of the ANSI/NISO Z39.48–1992 (Permanence of Paper)

ISBN: 978-1-60732-971-8 (paperback)
ISBN: 978-1-60732-972-5 (ebook)
https://doi.org/10.7330/9781607329725

Library of Congress Cataloging-in-Publication Data

Names: Harris, Joseph (Joseph D.), author.
Title: The work of teaching writing : learning from fiction, film, and drama / by Joseph Harris.
Description: Logan : Utah State University Press, [2019] | Includes bibliographical references and index.
Identifiers: LCCN 2019052097 (print) | LCCN 2019052098 (ebook) | ISBN 9781607329718 (paperback) | ISBN 9781607329725 (ebook)
Subjects: LCSH: Teachers in motion pictures. | Teachers in literature.
Classification: LCC PN1995.9.T4 H37 2019 (print) | LCC PN1995.9.T4 (ebook) | DDC 791.43/6557—dc23
LC record available at https://lccn.loc.gov/2019052097
LC ebook record available at https://lccn.loc.gov/2019052098

Cover illustration © eelke dekker/Flickr

For my fellow writing teachers

CONTENTS

ACKNOWLEDGMENTS

I thank the Edwin Mellen Press for permission to reprint, in chapter 1, several paragraphs of my piece "Dead Poets and Wonder Boys: Writing Teachers in the Movies," which first appeared in *How "The Teacher" Is Presented in Literature, History, Religion, and the Arts*, edited by Raymond McCluskey and Stephen J. McKinney (2013). I owe special thanks to Raymond and Stephen for hosting the lively and amiable International Conference on Representations of the Teacher at the University of Glasgow, Scotland, in July 2008, which was the moment when I first began thinking seriously about the issues in this book. I also thank Utah State University Press for permission to reprint, in chapter 3, my analysis of the exchanges between Wilfred Owen and Siegfried Sassoon, which first appeared in the second edition of my book *A Teaching Subject* (2012).

I had the chance while I was at Duke University to teach several undergraduate seminars on representations of teaching and learning. I particularly remember a moment in one of them when I had asked the class what we saw students and teachers actually *doing* in the texts we were reading and watching together, and they replied "well, we almost never see them doing any real work." That comment stayed with me, and I hope it is clear how it has informed my writing.

It was my close friend and co-teacher at the University of Pittsburgh, Steve Carr, who first pointed out to me that Phaedrus asks Socrates to *remind* him (rather than help him *remember*) what they've been discussing. I asked another friend, the classicist Peter Burian of Duke University, to check if this shift in verbs was an accident of translation, and he assured me it was not. I don't presume that either Steve or Peter will agree with my eccentric reading of the *Phaedrus*, but I could never have constructed it without them.

Julie Wilson found many of the critical texts I discuss in Background Readings during the summer she worked as my research assistant. She has helped me look more learned (or, at least, sort of). I am very thankful. Jeanne Marie Rose of Penn State Berks and Margaret DeBelius of Georgetown University offered very useful responses to the first draft of this manuscript, pushing me to make the line of thought that connects my readings of various texts more clear. And out of the blue, Paul Corrigan of Southeastern University generously offered to read the near-final version of this book and helped me formulate my title, a new introduction, and the line of thinking they gesture toward. I owe him special thanks. I am also grateful to have had the chance to informally share my work in progress with too many friends and colleagues to list here, most of whom asked: Did you ever read this? Or, did you ever watch that? I always hurried to do the newly assigned reading or viewing.

Dan Pratt has designed a handsome and bold cover for this book. My thanks to him. I also owe thanks to Cheryl Carnahan for her close and attentive copyediting of my manuscript, to Laura Furney for establishing the format of the book, and to Linda Gregonis for preparing its index. And it was a special pleasure to have the help of Rachael Levay, the new acquisitions editor at Utah State University Press, in turning my manuscript into a book. Rachael is stepping into the shoes of one of the great editors of books on teaching writing, Michael Spooner, and she is doing so with grace and authority.

I walked into and out of writing this book several times over the last decade. Art is long, and life is short. So I am grateful to my wife, Pat, for turning to me at breakfast one morning and asking "so, are you going to finish that book this summer?" I offer her all my thanks and love.

THE WORK OF
TEACHING WRITING

A book is a machine to think with . . .
—I. A. Richards

INTRODUCTION

Teaching writing is not a glamorous job. Our days are occupied with essays and books, classes and committees and office hours. If there is an image that sums up what we are about, then it must be the stack of student papers waiting to be read and commented on, set next to the laptop alongside the pens, post-its, folders, and coffee cups cluttering the desk. Ours is a busy if quiet line of work, bookish by definition, filled with words and ideas more than actions.

And yet writing teachers are familiar figures in the popular imagination—playing key roles in novels like *Push*, *Up the Down Staircase*, and *Old School*, movies like *Dead Poets Society*, *Freedom Writers*, and *Educating Rita*, and plays like *Oleanna* and *The History Boys*. As a college writing teacher, I'm interested in what such books, movies, and plays have to tell me about my work. How do others understand what I am trying to accomplish? How do they represent the experience of learning to write? How can I draw on the scenes and stories they offer in rethinking my own work with student writers?

Before outlining my plan for answering those questions, let me quickly note two things this book is *not*. First, it is not a critique. There is a long tradition of complaint among academics about how our work has been represented in popular culture. The usual criticism is that popular books and movies tend to sentimentalize good teaching as hinging on an ability to connect with students as persons and very little else. And so, as one academic critic after the other has pointed out, teacher features tend to gloss over real problems of gender, race, class, and authority in the classroom, since the only thing that really matters, it would seem, is that the teacher *cares*. The professional,

DOI: 10.7330/9781607329725.c000

the political, and the intellectual are all subsumed by the personal. We are left with a popular view of the ideal teacher as the friend and hero of students that many real-life teachers find almost impossible to accept.

There is much that is admirable about this scrupulous refusal of a flattering image of ourselves. There is also something off-putting about it. For when we resist the role of the teacher as the person who cares, who inspires, who goes the extra mile to reach students, we are in effect telling the rest of the culture that, once again, they've got it wrong, that they should really want a *different* sort of teacher. We do not, it quickly becomes clear, much appreciate having others tell us how to do our work. By distancing ourselves from the images of teachers in the media, we reassert our authority over what should count as good teaching.

For an example, we might turn to Dale Bauer's smart and influential 1998 essay, "Indecent Proposals," about how college teachers are depicted in movies. Bauer begins by discussing *The Mirror Has Two Faces* (1996), a Hollywood romance in which Barbra Streisand, improbably cast as an Ivy League professor, vamps and flirts her way through a set of lectures to infatuated undergraduates. What might we as teachers have to learn from this campy portrayal of our work? Not much, it turns out. Instead Bauer argues that what we really need to do is explain to viewers how such movies misrepresent our work, thereby "redeeming our own images from the trivialization they suffer on film" (315). The real lesson is thus not for us as teachers but for the culture at large—which has once again confused the political with the personal and the personal with the erotic, so that our teaching "is now represented as a sexual proposition" (302).

But can we only learn from popular texts about teaching by resisting what they have to say? Teaching is indeed difficult and complex intellectual work; it should not be reduced to a simple matter of effort and caring. Fair enough. But while such criticisms are correct, they are also familiar and easy. For instance, one of the very first episodes of the witty TV sitcom *Community* begins with a hyper-animated community college teacher who, like John Keating in *Dead Poets Society,* urges his class to stand on their desks to see the world anew. "Why not?" he shouts. As if in response, one of the cheap, plastic-and-metal, prefab school desks comes crashing down under the weight of the student teetering on it. "She's okay. Go to the nurse. Seize the day" fusses the professor, quickly dismissing the class ("Introduction to Film," 2009).

But if TV sitcoms are already mocking the loopy, earnest passion of teachers in the movies, then we would hardly seem to need academic critics to belabor the point. Besides, there seems less to gain from describing what's wrong with popular images of teaching than from trying to glean some lessons from them. Or to put all this another way, my hope is that the texts I look at in this book will serve not only as objects of analysis but also, as I. A. Richards put it, as *machines to think with* (2001 [1924], 7). What I find most useful in Richards's phrase is not the noun—although do I like the idea of a text as a machine or tool—but the preposition: What might it mean to think not just *about* a text but *with* it?

Second, I don't have much to say here about the crowded and pleasurable genre of the academic novel—with its depictions of the twists and turns of professorial careers, rivalries and affairs, campus intrigues, and even occasional murders. There's been a good bit written about such fiction already; Elaine Showalter's *Faculty Towers* (2005) is a fairly recent and representative example. To my eyes, her study mirrors not only the appeal but the limits of its subject. It is perceptive, witty, and learned—but almost completely uninterested in the actual work of teaching. We usually see the faculty in academic novels as they circulate from their book-lined studies to conference halls, administrative meeting rooms, cafés, bars, and bedrooms (often not their own)—interrupted by only an occasional visit or two to a classroom. All that is part of their escapist allure. But while, like many professors, I'm a fan of the academic novel, my focus here lies to the side of this genre, since my interest is not in books or movies about academics per se but in depictions of teachers and students at work together on writing.

Hence my title: *The Work of Teaching Writing*. There are hundreds of novels, plays, and films that deal in some way with either writing teachers or students. My interest is in the much smaller number that show them at work together. This has involved me looking for texts that imagine the actual writing done by students. In novels this often means "reproducing" what a student has written, although, of course, the novelist has to first write the text before quoting it—as when we read Precious's journals in *Push* or the stories of the students in *The Writing Class*. In movies and plays, such moments often involve a character reading aloud from a student paper—as in *Oleanna, Freedom Writers*, or *Educating Rita*. I am drawn to how such scenes frame a key moment in teaching. A student writes something. A response is called for. The teacher can no longer simply inspire, exhort, lecture, or entertain; they now have to do some real work.

In the chapters that follow, I look at how that work has been depicted in current novels, films, and plays. I believe that as teachers of writing we have something to learn from studying not just theories of discourse or rhetoric or pedagogy but also stories that depict the lived experience of teaching. I suspect that most of us who decide to continue to teach writing throughout our careers do so, in strong part, because we enjoy the actual doing of it—the assigning and planning and commenting and talking—as the work unfolds from class to class, week to week, semester to semester. I want to see what imaginative texts can show us about that experience.

In chapter 1, "Dead Poets and Wonder Boys," I try to set the tone of this approach by looking at what we might learn when we take a generous rather than a skeptical view of how recent movies have depicted the teaching of writing. I argue that there's much to gain from shifting our focus from how teachers are portrayed to how the actual work of teaching is dramatized. And so the films I end up finding most compelling are those—like *Educating Rita* or *Misery*—that show teachers not simply inspiring students to write but actually responding to what they have to say. I'm interested in moments of conversation, of back-and-forth exchange.

In the next few chapters, I look at how the work of teaching has been depicted at different stages of the writing process. In chapter 2, "Beginnings," I turn to how several playwrights and novelists have represented the problem of helping students take on what are, for them, new ways of writing. One of the texts I look at closely is Alan Bennett's marvelous play *The History Boys* (2006), in which we encounter a student who wants to know which of his teachers he most needs to please—the one who wants a reflective and "thoughtful" response from him or the one who wants him to be surprising and "smart." But the real challenge for student writers runs even deeper. They need to figure how to enter into a new discourse, how to become thoughtful or smart or anything else, without having to check the persons they used to be at the door. Another text I look at, David Mamet's *Oleanna* (1993), dramatizes the painful failure of a student to do so—and of a teacher to help her. But two classic novels of teaching in New York City—Bel Kaufman's *Up the Down Staircase* (1964) and Sapphire's *Push* (1996)—offer us some powerful insights into how teachers can build on the ways with words students bring with them to school. Both books suggest that to challenge students we must first respect them.

In chapter 3, "Work in Progress," I look at several scenes from novels in which a teacher helps a student develop a piece of writing. These are scenes that focus not on the beginning stages of drafting a text but on the later work of revising it. The key issues center around agency. How much should students defer to the authority of their teacher as they make changes to a text? When should teachers insist on their expertise? Several books and plays imagine this relationship in terms of erotic submission: The student must become not only the teacher's disciple but also their lover. Others view the relationship more as one of master and apprentice—as when, for example, in the novels of both Jincy Willet and William Coles, a gruff taskmaster of a teacher leads students through their paces while still demanding they produce original work. And most hopefully, a few novels—Pat Barker's *Regeneration* (1992), Antonio Skármeta's

The Postman (1985/1995)—imagine the teaching of writing as the slow development of a friendship, a collaboration.

I continue this exploration in chapter 4, "Forging a Self," where I look at four remarkable novels that center on what happens when doubt infects the working relationship between student and teacher, writer and reader. The plots of Curtis Sittenfeld's *Prep* (2005), Francine Proses's *Blue Angel* (2000), May Sarton's *The Small Room* (1961), and Tobias Wolff's *Old School* (2004) all hinge on instances of deception in writing—and yet in each case we are made to feel sympathy for the young person who has chosen to deceive or plagiarize. These four novels suggest that a sense of self is not something that already exists, that a writer needs simply to express in their prose, but something that must be achieved, created, earned. They also show how teachers can hinder the attempts of students to forge this sense of self on the page when they present themselves as models rather than coworkers. But they also offer a more optimistic view of the teaching of writing that is founded on a close attention both to craft and to the person behind those words.

In chapter 5, "The Limits of Rhetoric," I take a step back from this close analysis of students, teachers, and texts. For the first time in this book, I look closely at two imaginative works that do not feature "student papers." And yet, ironically, both of these works present themselves quite literally as lessons in rhetoric, in writing. The first text is Plato's *Phaedrus* (1995). This is also a step back in another sense, since unlike the other works I look at, which have all been composed in the last 50 years or so, Plato's dialogue is about 2,400 years old and remains a foundational, philosophical text. But still, and whatever else it might be, the *Phaedrus* is also an extraordinary one-act play that presents a conversation between a student and teacher that seems, to my ears at least, uncannily similar to those that go on in many writing classrooms today. The second text is Peter Dimock's *A Short Rhetoric for Leaving the Family*, a moving novella whose troubled narrator reworks yet another classical rhetorical treatise, the *Rhetorica ad Herennium*, in a flailing attempt to come to terms with his family's involvement in the Vietnam War. In my view, both Plato and Dimock end up showing that teaching writing cannot be reduced to the presentation of a general system, that teachers must instead root their work in the particular aims of the students they are working with. (I'm convinced that Dimock does so purposefully; about Plato, I can't say.) In that sense, the *Phaedrus* and *A Short Rhetoric* argue for an attention to student work. They suggest, that is, that the teaching of writing is grounded not in presentation but in careful listening and response.

. Why, then, is it so hard to do well? In my postscript, "On the Job," I look at three recent novels—Julie Schumacher's *Dear Committee Members* (2015), Richard Russo's *Straight Man* (1997), and James Hynes's *The Lecturer's Tale* (2001)—that highlight the routinely oppressive workloads of most writing teachers. Each of these novels offers a ground-level view of how difficult it is for good teaching to flourish in bad working conditions. Unless you're a hero or a martyr or very lucky, it's almost certain that there will always be more students with a claim on your attention than you have time and energy to offer. These books hint that what we need are not better theories of rhetoric so much as better ways of offering teachers the time and support they need to do their work with thought and passion.

In focusing on depictions of students and teachers at work together, I hope to call attention to such everyday aspects of teaching writing. I am aware that the material contexts of that labor are rapidly shifting—as less and less of the work of teaching now involves, in a digital age, a student and teacher looking together at words on a page. We are as likely to be exchanging online responses to video essays as scribbling comments in the margins of student papers. But I think the dynamic Plato dramatized in the *Phaedrus* still holds. A student produces some work. A teacher responds. Together they try to formulate some insights into writing. My aim here is to see what fiction, film, and drama can tell us about that moment, that exchange.

When I began this project, I thought I'd find a fair number of similar studies to consult—given that the teaching of writing still takes place, for the most part, in English departments, which are filled with people who are also teaching about stories, plays, and films. But that hasn't proved to be the case. There's a good bit of writing just to the side of my interests—studies of the academic novel, articles about individual texts or authors—and I briefly review that scholarship in a closing section on background readings. But as for tracing how novels, plays, and films have imagined teachers *at work* with students on their writing—there, for the most part, I've needed to chart my own course.

Perhaps not surprisingly, then, the line of thought I pursue in this book is not always straight. I've let my thinking follow the lead of the texts I've read and watched. But I hope that in doing so I've also been able to make the case that while teaching writing does indeed depend on connecting with students as individuals, this connection needs to be made on an *intellectual* level. What distinguishes the teaching of writing is that our ideas come to life in the work of our students. My goal is to think with some novels, movies, and plays to see how we can make that happen.

1

DEAD POETS AND
WONDER BOYS

A friend of mine who teaches anthropology loves the *Raiders of the Lost Ark* movies. Who cares if they're unrealistic, he says; how can you not like seeing yourself as Indiana Jones? Writing teachers also appear surprisingly often in the movies, frequently in heroic roles. The charismatic John Keating of *Dead Poets Society*, the gutsy Erin Gruwell of *Freedom Writers*, the caring William Forrester of *Finding Forrester*, the winsome Grady Tripp of *Wonder Boys*. Such movies show us teachers who change the lives of students through writing. So you might think that most real-life writing teachers would applaud these flattering versions of who we are and what we do. But, in fact, many of us feel impatient with such films. The idealized versions of teaching they offer seem at once unattainable and off-target. In the midst of all their jumping on desks and running after troubled students, we rarely see movie teachers get down to the actual labor of commenting on student drafts or preparing for the next day's classes. The hard and ordinary work of teaching writing—the work we know and value—gets lost in the larger-than-life heroics of movie teachers.

But do we really want to begrudge such a positive view of teaching? After all, do the movies offer a realistic view of any profession? And if most of us can't hope to be as funny and passionate as John Keating or as devoted to students as Erin Gruwell, doesn't it seem a little self-serving to argue that good teaching doesn't really hinge on such qualities? It's easy enough to criticize the heroic view of the teacher such movies present. The question is what to offer in its place.

DOI: 10.7330/9781607329725.c001

In this opening chapter, I look at the problems raised by the writing teacher as movie hero to clear some space for another way of thinking about how our work has been depicted by non-academics. In my view we can learn more from movie versions of our work if we spend less time asking about how they portray us as professionals and more about how they depict the intellectual labor of teaching. *From teacher to teaching*. We need to look for those moments in films when teachers and students work together on writing and see what we can learn from what goes on in them.

But first I want to look at the two main ways the movies have presented writing teachers. On the one hand, there is the teacher as hero—exemplified by John Keating in *Dead Poets Society* and Erin Gruwell in *Freedom Writers*—who works energetically to inspire students to find their own voices as writers. On the other hand, there is the teacher as a burned-out case—Grady Tripp in *Wonder Boys*, Frank in *Educating Rita*, William in *Finding Forrester*—who is himself in need of rescue, blocked as both a writer and a feeling person. And there is strikingly little else in between. The dead poets and wonder boys of film thus end up testifying to the limits of imagining the success of teaching as hinging on the person, the charisma of the teacher.

PLODDERS, DILETTANTES, NOVICES

But before I turn to those dead poets and wonder boys, let me point quickly to a few other glimpses of writing teachers in the movies. None of these scenes appear in movies about teaching; rather, the point of each is provide some backstory, to offer insight into the makeup of a leading character by revealing that he or she teaches writing. All of them strike me as deft, comic, and realistic—even if none presents our field as we might hope.

The first comes from *Saving Private Ryan*, Stephen Spielberg's 1998 film recounting a mission behind enemy lines to rescue an American soldier during the D-Day invasion. The leader of this mission, Captain John Miller (Tom Hanks), is a figure of awe and fascination to the soldiers in his platoon, who have a running bet to see who can guess what Miller's job back home is. Of course, none of them can, and the secret is not revealed until a tense moment midway through the film when Miller's field sergeant (Tom Sizemore) finds himself in a fierce argument with one of his own soldiers. A pistol is pointed and threats are shouted until the captain breaks in to ask, "What's the pool on me up to?" Having thus seized the startled attention of his company, he quietly tells them, "I'm a schoolteacher. I teach English composition."

Clearly, no one has guessed this occupation. The sergeant, pistol still in hand, turns toward the camera and mutters, "I'll be doggone." The situation is defused. The war hero has revealed himself as a regular guy, with as mundane a stateside job as can be imagined. As Captain Miller himself goes on to say:

> Back home, I tell people what I do for a living, and they go, that figures. But here . . . here everything is a big mystery. So I guess I've changed. (*Saving Private Ryan* 1:39)[1]

It's a familiar war-movie scene: adversity calls forth greatness from an ordinary man. Of course, what makes the scene stand out for me, though, is the wry jolt of self-recognition it prompts. In searching for a job that would instantly peg its holder as undistinguished, earnest, and banal—the filmmakers came up with my own.

But if teaching English composition signifies a prior life of quiet dullness for John Miller, it is intended to point out something else altogether about Annie Savoy, the siren of minor-league baseball played by Susan Sarandon in Ron Shelton's 1988 *Bull Durham*. Annie is an artsy, flighty, talkative flirt who each summer, as a kind of erotic hobby, seduces a new ball-player on the Durham Bulls, the minor-league baseball team in her southern hometown. In the summer in which the film is set, though, she finds herself torn between a promising young pitcher and a veteran catcher, Crash Davis, played by Kevin Costner. Midway through the film, Annie and Crash fall into

---

1. Throughout this book, I will locate film scenes and quotations by the hour and minute they begin in the DVD or streaming version of the movie.

the sort of exasperated bickering that in romantic comedies is almost always the prelude to sex and love. Crash is clearly attracted to Annie but mocks her colorful clothing, assertive sexuality, and impromptu philosophizing as "a little excessive for the Carolina league." When Annie quotes William Blake in response ("The road of excess leads to the palace of wisdom"), Crash throws up his arms and says, "Who are you? I mean, do you even have a job?" To which Annie defiantly replies, "I teach part-time at Alamance Junior College, English 101 *and* beginning composition" (*Bull Durham* 1:10).

So again the answer to the question—what sort of job could this person possibly hold?—turns out to be teaching writing. But Annie Savoy is not a plodder like John Miller; she is, rather, an enthusiast and a bit of a scatterbrain—not someone who would be taken seriously as an intellectual or a "real" professor but still someone we can easily imagine teaching "beginning composition." As the director of a university writing program, I once asked an applicant for a part-time position teaching first-year writing why they were interested in the job, only to have them tell me that "it seems like something a reasonably well-educated person can do without much training." Annie Savoy is that sort of educated but untrained person. I'm aware that this scene from *Bull Durham* might perturb many women, southerners, two-year college faculty, and writing teachers. But that is pretty much the point. *Teaching composition* often operates as a punch line in our culture. Given that, I am intrigued that so much criticism in our field has been directed toward images that idealize our work.

But let me offer one more glimpse of the writing teacher—one I find accurate and endearing. In Alan J. Pakula's 1979 *Starting Over*, Burt Reynolds plays Phil Potter, an airline magazine writer who decides, as he begins a new life after a messy divorce, to get a job teaching college writing. And so we watch as Phil, dressed in a natty tweed jacket and slacks, cautiously approaches his first 9:00 a.m. class. After stalling for a moment at the water fountain, Phil enters the classroom and nervously introduces himself to about thirty chatty and distracted students. The clock on the wall behind him reads 9:02. A jump cut then shows Phil sitting behind a desk, in mid-sentence, telling the class "and so, the next time we meet, I'd like you to bring a magazine article that you like, and we'll discuss it." He then gathers his books and papers together and moves to leave. At that point, one of the students interjects, "Uh, Mr. Potter, the class doesn't end until ten." We look again at the clock. It is 9:04. Phil returns to his seat and says "good, that gives me a chance to answer all your questions for . . . the next fifty-six minutes" before sheepishly admitting that he will make sure to prepare more material for the next class (*Starting Over*, 0:43).

With a quick and empathetic wit, this scene surfaces one of the deepest anxieties of any teacher: that you will simply run out of things to say. It also hints that there might more to teaching writing than just knowing how to write. *Starting Over* never returns to the classroom, so we don't learn if or how Phil grows any better as a teacher. And certainly, in this brief comic scene, he seems a disastrous (if likable) combination of the plodding John Miller and the scattered Annie Savoy. But we do get a sense, if only by inference, that there is craft to teaching that Phil has yet to learn. I've seen few other movies that suggest as much.

Plodders, dilettantes, novices. These are familiar and uncontroversial images of writing teachers. But then things start to get bad. The movies start to show us as heroes.

DEAD POETS

Academic critics have pointed to a remarkably consistent and troubling image of the teacher in the movies. They argue that in portraying the good teacher as an iconoclast who struggles against an uncaring system, Hollywood ends up depicting most educators as incompetents or functionaries—as the dead wood in the faculty lounge or the drones in the head office. The profession is damned as a few heroic exceptions to its norms are praised. Teacher features thus tend to follow a kind of Wild West narrative—as the lone teacher strides into school, stares down bureaucrats, stands up to troublemakers, and speaks out for students.

The archetypical rendering of the teacher as hero is Peter Weir's 1988 *Dead Poets Society*. Critics of how teachers have been shown in movies—William Ayers (1994), Kevin Dettmar (2014), and Henry Giroux (2002) among them—have returned over and over to this film with a sort of dread fascination. (I realize I am adding to that list here.) Set in the 1950s at a New England prep school for boys, *Dead Poets* chronicles the efforts of a young English teacher, John Keating, to get his students to see books and ideas not as mere schoolwork but as the stuff of life. *Carpe diem* is his motto and Walt Whitman his hero. Much of the power of the film comes from the bravura performance of Robin Williams as Mr. Keating. Because, really, who wouldn't want Robin Williams as an English teacher? And Keating does indeed inspire many students, who take on his tastes and enthusiasms, forming the Dead Poets Society, a group that meets secretly at night to smoke, drink, and talk about poetry, music, girls, and life—kind of a teenage version of bohemia. But Keating's irreverent manner also rankles many colleagues and parents, and when one of his students commits suicide, this is used as a pretext to fire him.

Unlike many movies in which the profession of a character is used simply as color or backstory, *Dead Poets Society* is fascinated by Keating *as a teacher*. Indeed, we learn very little about Keating outside of his role in the classroom. I suspect that this forms a strong part of the film's appeal. The man is the work; for John Keating, teaching is not a job but an avocation.

Three scenes in the first half of the movie define what it sees as the genius of Keating's teaching. The first comes on the opening day of school, when Keating leads the students out of their classroom and into a hallway, where they gaze at display cases filled with trophies and photos from the past—only to be reminded by Keating that these were all won by boys who, though once young like them, have long since grown old and died. "We are food for worms, lads . . . Seize the day!" he whispers urgently to them (0:11). Talking among themselves as they leave this first class, the students pronounce Keating "weird, but different." The next scene occurs when Keating denounces a stuffy critical preface to the class poetry anthology as "excrement" and orders his students to rip those pages from their books—which they do tentatively at first but soon with abandon, tossing the torn-out pages into a wastebasket that Keating, egging them on, carries about the room (0:21). The third and most famous (or notorious) scene shows Keating leaping onto his desk in the middle of a class lecture in order, as he tells his students, "to remind myself that we must constantly look at things in a different way." He then directs them to climb, one by one, onto his desk, to look around for themselves before jumping back down again. Once each of them has done so, he tells the class that their next assignment, due on Monday, is to "compose a poem of your own, an original work" (0:43).

The episodes following this third scene are the only ones in the movie in which we watch a student actually trying to do some schoolwork. They show us Todd Anderson (Ethan Hawke), an earnest student who clearly wants to answer Keating's call to write his own verse, as he struggles to compose a poem. We see a loose-leaf page filled with scribbling and scratch-outs, which Todd hides from his friends, and, finally, a late-night moment of anguish as he crumples up the paper he has been working on all day and tosses it away. The next morning in class, we first watch one student read a mediocre love poem, which Keating praises, and then another who reads a juvenile couplet, which Keating excuses. Then he turns to Todd, who has nothing. Keating leads him to the front of the class, where he demands that Todd utter a Whitmanesque "barbaric yawp." Then he circles Todd, prodding and cajoling him before the class, somehow coaxing a spontaneous and improbable stream of free verse from the boy. Overcome, Keating embraces Todd in the front of the room, telling him "don't you forget this" (0:57).

But what has actually happened? Todd has learned little about how to write a poem, except perhaps to howl in anxious if eloquent pain. Keating never shows any interest in or awareness of his student's drafts, cross-outs, and revisions. The lesson he teaches is less in writing than in living. What he has to offer is himself. And that he does repeatedly. Throughout *Dead Poets Society*, students do whatever Keating tells them to—leaning expectantly toward the display case to hear voices from the past, ripping the pages out of their books, jumping onto a desk and off of it ("like lemmings," as even Keating notes), marching in unison when he orders and strutting eccentrically when he tells them otherwise. In between, they gaze mutely at their teacher—in one rapt close-up after the other. But they also form a society to talk about books and ideas, write poetry and play music, and question authority. What they are learning, that is, for both good and bad, is how to be like John Keating.

I don't think I know of a teaching movie whose reception has been more divided than *Dead Poets Society*. When I talk about the film with teachers, I can rely on hearing one of them say at some point, "I'm not jumping up on *my* desk." But when I talk with students, I get the strong sense that they wish more of us might. If the stance of academics toward the film has been consistently skeptical or even hostile, most popular reviews of the film on its release were enthusiastic, including those by serious critics like Stanley Kaufmann (1989) and Pauline Kael (1989), and *Dead Poets Society* continues to receive high marks on internet fan sites. The film was nominated for several Academy Awards in 1990 and won for Best Screenplay (by Tom Schulman). I still recall the evening I first went to see *Dead Poets Society* and felt the crowd of moviegoers around me respond with laughter and warmth to scenes that made me shift uneasily in my seat. I've taught the film several times since—and many students have greeted it as an old favorite, while new viewers have almost always cited it as a highlight of the semester. And almost everyone I've talked with about my work on this book has soon mentioned *Dead Poets Society*.

The difference is that most non-teachers say they really like the movie and most teachers say they don't. Let me be clear. I agree with the critics of *Dead Poets Society*. You can't simply tell new teachers that their job is to be unorthodox and alluring. Most of us aren't up to such a task, and even if we were, the aim of teaching shouldn't be to foster a cult of personality. Still, though, I think we need not simply to resist but to build upon the attraction of *Dead Poets Society*. What does the film promise its viewers that is so powerful? Is there any way real teachers can deliver on that promise?

Dead Poets Society strives to connect the world of ideas and books to everyday life. In this film, reading and writing *matter*. Invoking Whitman, Keating tells his students, huddled around him in the classroom, that "the powerful play goes on, and you may contribute a verse" (0:26). That is powerful stuff, and the film's many close-up shots of students gazing awestruck at Keating reinforce the message. But the weakness of Keating's pedagogy is that it sticks at the level of exhortation. Keating inspires, incites, provokes, but we don't see him doing any actual work with students as they struggle to develop their voices as writers.

Rather than reject Keating, then, I think we need to continue his work, to push it a step further—to argue that a good teacher not only encourages students to talk, write, and question but also helps them do all those things better. The problem with John Keating as a teacher is not that he is impossibly charismatic and inspirational but that he is *only* charismatic and inspirational. Similarly, the problem with *Dead Poets Society* is not that it misrepresents teachers but that it shows such little interest in the work of students. We can out-Keating Keating. We can tell students that, like John Keating, we care deeply about what they have to say but that, unlike him, we are willing to demonstrate this care in how we work with them as writers.

The figure of the dead poet has recurred in movies about teaching since the 1950s. Rick Dadier in *Blackboard Jungle* (1955), Mark Thackeray in *To Sir, with Love* (1967), Sylvia Barrett in *Up the Down Staircase* (1967), Katherine Anne Watson in *Mona Lisa Smile* (2003), Erin Gruwell in *Freedom Writers* (2007). These are movies about young and passionate teachers who buck the system, connect with students, and work hard and selflessly on their behalf. But while there's good reason to be skeptical of a view of teaching that stops there, as all of these movies do, we also need to acknowledge its power. Dead poets succeed as teachers because they earn the trust and affection of students. While such movies may mistake a starting point of teaching for its end, we slight that starting point at our peril. It may well be that you can't teach writing without first connecting with writers.

In an insightful piece titled "The Professors of History," the film scholar Dana Polan (1996) notes how movies tend to caricature science professors as socially inept geniuses who are more at home with their computers and lab equipment than with other people. Still, Polan observes, scientists are also imagined in the movies as having access to arcane and useful forms of knowledge, of being able to create monsters and cures, theorems and rocket ships. Humanities professors, on the other hand, are rarely shown in the movies as possessing any sort of specialized knowledge. What they know about instead is people, feeling, life. Urbane and charming, their effects are felt not on the world but on the minds—and often the bodies—of students. In contrast to the dispassionate inquiry of science, the teaching of literature and writing is portrayed as a kind of dance or seduction. Scientists study the world; humanists move students. (Polan goes on in his essay to argue that the movies show history professors as caught in the middle, lacking both the authority of scientists and the personal magnetism of humanists.)

The dead poet embodies this charged and dynamic view of humanist teaching. It is striking how much of movie pedagogy is physical. Teacher features are filled with out-of-class excursions and events—trips to museums and ball fields, guest speakers, parties, dances, bake sales. And the dead poet as teacher is almost always shown in motion. Keating strides about his classroom and leaps upon the furniture. The turning point of *Freedom Writers* comes when Erin Gruwell dares students to step up to a line she has taped down the middle of the classroom. Later she dances, clumsily but enthusiastically, with them. The manly heroes of *Blackboard Jungle* and *To Sir, with Love* have cathartic fistfights with bullies that earn them the respect of other students. And *To Sir, with Love* ends with a stiff but affectionate dance between teacher and student, Sidney Poitier and Lulu. While some of all this activity might be traced back to the simple need to keep things moving onscreen, I suspect there is more to it than that. Dead poet movies insist on linking ideas to bodies and actions.

A key task of the dead poet as teacher, then, is to set students in motion. And so, while we rarely watch dead poets *respond* to student work, we often see them *assign* it. In *Freedom Writers*, for instance, we watch and listen as Erin Gruwell (played by Hillary Swank) describes, patiently and in considerable detail, how she wants students to write in the copybooks she is giving them as journals, what she will or will not read, where the books will be stored, and so on. It's actually quite a lot of teacher-talk to sit through for a popular movie, but then the pace quickens. We soon read with Gruwell (through voice-over) the spontaneous, movingly detailed, and seemingly unedited stories her students write in their journals. And then we watch as they work on computers to transcribe those handwritten journal entries into the stories that will become the *Freedom Writers* book. (Many of these stories were incorporated into a 2007 spin-off book, edited by the actual Erin Gruwell whose work as a teacher inspired the movie.) Throughout this process, Gruwell cheers students on and lobbies school bureaucrats for support. But at no point do we see her offer students advice about how to shape their stories or translate their experiences into language. Her intellectual work as a teacher, that is, seems to come to an end once she has given students a reason to write.

But that was always Gruwell's aim—to inspire, to help students see that they have something to say. To move students, dead poets have to entertain, to perform. They are not anti-intellectual; on the contrary, they want to excite students about writing and ideas. But neither do they seem much interested in the details of actual intellectual work. Dead poets are young, attractive, energetic, committed, irreverent—in a word, sexy. But the question is unavoidable: What happens as the dead poet grows old?

WONDER BOYS

The Prime of Miss Jean Brodie, directed by Robert Neame (1968), is a haunting study of the personal consequences—for both students and teacher—of a pedagogy based on charisma. Set in a small Edinburgh school for girls in the years leading up to World War II, the film is based on the short and acute novel by Muriel Spark (1962) and, with some small changes to characters and plot, retains Spark's unflinching portrait of Jean Brodie as a teacher and person. As played by Maggie Smith, Miss Jean Brodie is a stunning, intelligent, unmarried woman in her self-described prime, which is to say she is no longer quite young—in her early forties, it would seem. Unconventional and worldly, she is mentor to the "Brodie set"—a group of four ambitious girls, labeled by Brodie as "the crème de la crème," who, fascinated by their teacher, strive to adopt her tastes, first in art and literature and then, as they move through their teens, in politics, men, and sex.

The vain Brodie thrives on their emulation. But her influences are ambiguous at best, as she encourages one student toward fascist politics and another toward an affair with an older man. But the movie is also about the cruelty of youth, as one of Brodie's protégés quietly usurps her position, both personal and professional—by taking on one of her teacher's lovers as her own and then intriguing to have Brodie dismissed from the school faculty. It is as if to fully impersonate her teacher, the student must also replace her.

The Prime of Miss Jean Brodie thus reveals a dark side of teaching as courtship or seduction. On the one hand, the more charismatic the teacher, the stronger will be her sway over students. On the other hand, the student must at some point pull away from the teacher—and the more intense the bond between the two, the harsher this rejection must seem. Few other books or movies have gazed so steadily at this tense relationship between youth and age. *Brodie* documents the perils of growing old as a teacher, as both novel and film close with Jean Brodie left discredited and alone. But there has also emerged a small genre of films that offer a far more romantic view of, as it were, the dead poet past his prime.

The protagonist of these movies is most often a man in late middle age, a onetime rebel who over the years has grown bored as a teacher and blocked as a writer. A good example is Professor Grady Tripp (Michael Douglass) in Curtis Hanson's *Wonder Boys* (2000). Tripp is unshaven, unkempt, often stoned, and seemingly unprepared for the one class we see him teach. He is hopelessly stuck on the writing of a big novel that is supposed to seal his reputation as a major author, infatuated with one of his undergraduate students, envious of the talents of another, about to be divorced from his second wife, and conducting an open affair with the chancellor of his school. He is, in short, a mess. We meet him at the start of the movie as he distractedly leads a creative writing workshop that has gone off the rails—the students hate a lugubrious story written by one of their fellows, and Tripp seems unable to do much besides wander about the classroom futilely urging them to "be constructive."

At the same time, Tripp is too likable not to be redeemed. He refuses to seduce the young woman in his class who fascinates him and who would clearly go to bed with him; he respects the skill and drive of the difficult young man whose story is trashed in the opening scene and helps him find a publisher; he realizes that he actually does love the chancellor and marries her—and through all this, he finds a way to start writing again. Even if the youthful enthusiasm and energy of the dead poet have faded into ironic detachment, the wonder boy still possesses empathy, wit, and an unused reserve of talent.

Second books and second chances dot the narratives of wonder boy movies. So do brilliant protégés. In Gus Van Sant's *Finding Forrester* (2000), the reclusive writer William Forrester (Sean Connery) is drawn back into the world by a chance encounter with Jamal, an African American teenager who is attending a New York City prep school on a basketball scholarship but whose real ambition is to write. The author of a single, much-celebrated novel, William agrees to tutor Jamal, who unsurprisingly proves to be an immensely fluent and eloquent writer. All William really needs to do is sit him down to work.

But then, when a skeptical teacher accuses Jamal of plagiarism, the agoraphobic William agrees unexpectedly to give a reading at the prep school. The faculty assumes that William is reading from a handwritten draft of his long-awaited second novel. Only after they have finished applauding does William reveal that the passage was actually written by Jamal. But there is a further twist, as at the end of the film we learn that William has in fact written another novel, dedicated to Jamal. Forrester has indeed been found—reawakened, rediscovered—through the process of teaching Jamal.

Similarly, in Lewis Gilbert's 1983 *Educating Rita*, Frank, an ex-poet and indifferent English tutor, is rejuvenated by Rita, a young ladies' hairdresser from Liverpool who comes to him as an Open University student. Based on the 1980 play by Willy Russell, *Educating Rita* is one of very few movies to include scenes of the actual work of teaching and learning—about which I'll have more to say later. Still, its storyline has a familiar arc. At the start of the film, Frank (Michael Caine) is charming, rumpled, cynical, and usually drunk. He has given up on both writing and teaching. But working with the unschooled but perspicuous Rita (Julie Walters) convinces him that he might still have something to say. The movie ends with him heading off to Australia to make a new start. Once again, the –*ing* in the film's title is important. Rita is indeed educated by Frank, but she has an educating influence on him as well.

Other wonder boys in recent movies include Glenn Holland (Richard Dreyfuss), the composer who does not rediscover his art until he fully commits himself to his students, in *Mr. Holland's Opus* (1995) and Andrew Crocker-Harris (Albert Finney), the fatigued teacher of classics in *The Browning Version* (1994) who is reminded of his original love of learning at the very end of his career. Crocker-Harris is the anti-dead poet, whose last words to his students are an apology for having failed to offer them "sympathy, encouragement, and humanity." His character has become something of a figure unto himself, having been played over the years in film and TV remakes of *The Browning Version* by an unusually distinguished series of actors: Michael Redgrave

(1951), Peter Cushing (1955), John Gielgud (1958), Ian Holm (1985), as well as Finney (1994).

The self-deprecating maturity of the wonder boy offsets some of the cowboy zeal of the dead poet. He has been around the block a few times, has known disappointment, and is less an outsider to the system than a second- or third-stringer within it. A hard-won humility is key to his effectiveness as a teacher. But at bottom the wonder boy and dead poet are versions of the same character. Both teach through the force of personality. And both are imagined as forces of good. The dead poet and wonder boy teach students to become versions of themselves, and the movies about them idealize those selves. There is almost never a downside to their influence. (Jean Brodie is the telling exception.) When things do go wrong, it is always somehow the fault of others—of overbearing parents, indifferent administrators, demanding employers, skeptical friends or spouses.

There is an appealing candor, then, to the discomfort many teachers feel with these images of ourselves. We know that teaching is far more difficult, and the interactions between teachers and students more complex and fraught, than such movies suggest. In her fine 1999 study *Tales out of School*, Jo Keroes looks at how the relationship between teacher and student has been depicted in a wide range of novels, plays, and films. Keroes is particularly interested in the emotional and erotic undercurrents of teaching, and she inveighs against the common portrait of the teacher as a Pygmalion who shapes a student to satisfy his own ambitions and desires. Her readings of several of the movies I've discussed here have informed mine. She contrasts the sentimental uplift of *Dead Poets* with the cooler ironies of *Jean Brodie* and applauds how in *Educating Rita* the flirtation between Frank and Rita ends in a meeting not of bodies but of minds. Her focus throughout *Tales*, however, remains on the figure of the teacher—and there our approaches diverge. I am more interested in how movies have depicted the *work* of teaching.

In a brief but astute essay for the *Chronicle of Higher Education*, Melora Wolff (2002) suggests that in the movies, "The drama of language is replaced by psychological dramas that praise and reinforce popular ideas about writers and writing teachers." I'd argue that most critics of movies about teaching have made a similar mistake. We have fixed our gaze on how films depict us as professionals and concluded, unsurprisingly, that they've gotten us all wrong. I think that line of analysis has brought us to a dead end, that to move ahead we need to shift our attention from the image of the writing teacher to the work of teaching writing. Let me suggest what such a shift might entail.

THE WORK OF TEACHING WRITING

I've spent a good deal of my time over the past two decades observing other writing teachers at work. If a teacher I am about to visit asks me what I hope to see, I usually tell them that I'm more interested in what they do than in watching what their students do. In many classrooms, of course, the students don't really do much of anything—except listen to the teacher, take notes, or text their friends. And even in many seemingly good classes, they are asked to do very little beyond occasionally offering an opinion as part of a teacher-led discussion. I've sat in many classrooms and listened to students and teachers talk brightly together about a text they've all just read. But when I've asked the teacher afterward how this conversation might help students with the essays they were *writing* for the course, I've too often received a blank look or an anxious reply to the effect that they just hope the class will somehow get people thinking.

The movies love quick and voluble classroom conversations. Indeed, they often suggest that such moments are the very aim of teaching. Sylvia Barrett finally breaks through to her class in *Up the Down Staircase* when she engages them in a boisterous discussion of *A Tale of Two Cities* as it relates to current politics. Mark Thackeray turns his class around in *To Sir, with Love* when he begins to talk with students about their lives. And each one of John Keating's classes seems to lead to some new personal epiphany.

I don't object to lively class discussions. They're fun. But in focusing so intently on the individual class meeting as a social drama—as an isolated event that goes either well or badly—we risk losing track of how so much of learning to write needs to take place over a longer span of time. Here, then, are some other forms of intellectual work we might look for in the movies:

- *Students write.* We see (or hear) some of the actual texts students create.

- *Teachers respond.* We watch teachers acting not just as cheerleaders who urge students forward but as coaches who offer comments and advice on their work.

- *Students revise.* We see evidence of learning in the changes students make to their writing.

Such a shift in focus can help us find insights into teaching in some unexpected movies, as well as see new possibilities in more familiar teacher features. Let me offer an example of each.

While I have never come across it on a list of movies about teaching, Rob Reiner's 1990 horror film, *Misery*, has a lot to say about writing and how it is taught. The movie is an abbreviated but accurate retelling of Stephen King's 1988 novel. Almost all of the action takes place in a single room of a snowbound and isolated cabin in the Rockies, where Paul Sheldon (James Caan), author of a bestselling series of romantic potboilers, is held captive by his "Number One Fan," the insane and violent Annie Wilkes (Kathy Bates). Paul has been badly injured in a car crash, but that is now the least of his worries. For in his last novel, Paul had brought his series of romances to a halt by killing off their heroine, Misery Chastaine, so he could then turn his talents to writing what he considers more serious fiction. But Annie is outraged by Misery's fictional demise and sets Paul the task of writing a new novel in which he brings her back from the dead. So long as the novel progresses to her satisfaction, Annie will allow the lame and now drug-dependent Paul to live. Under her watchful eye, Paul grudgingly begins work on the manuscript of "Misery's Return," all the while plotting his vengeance and escape.

The movie thus sets up a macabre version of a writing class. Annie has given Paul an assignment to complete, along with a due date (before the snows melt and search parties can come looking for him). She even turns the room in which she holds him captive into what she calls a writer's "studio"—consisting of a card table, some Corrasable Bond paper, and an old typewriter with a missing n key. And like so many writing teachers before her, she will serve as the first and only reader of his new work. We watch Paul as he struggles to compose a text that meets Annie's standards, which prove surprisingly high, while still injecting slight twists of defiance into his prose. Much of King's novel reproduces the pages of "Misery's Return" as Paul types them out, while the movie has Annie offer spirited abstracts of what she reads. There is even a hint of collaboration, as Annie uses a pen to fill in the missing ns in Paul's typescript. But overshadowing all this is the utter power Annie holds over Paul. She does not need to inspire, she compels. It is no surprise, then, that when Paul finally gets the chance to strike back, he acts out a schoolboy fantasy of revenge and rape—hitting Annie over the head with the typewriter she has provided and choking her with the pages she has forced him to write.

If this seems a grim version of a course in writing, then that is what horror movies often do so well—reveal the violence lurking under everyday life and work. Teachers often wish they could just make students do what they want, and, like Paul, many students have no doubt imagined alternative uses for the texts their teachers require them to produce. But unlike any of the other films I've discussed so far, *Misery* also shows a student learning something about the actual craft of writing. When Annie first assigns Paul the writing of "Misery's Return," he approaches the task cynically. His previous novel had ended with Misery Chastaine dying in childbirth. Convinced that Annie, whom he regards as a dupe like the rest of his readers, will accept almost any plot twist he comes up with, Paul opens his first draft of "Misery's Return" by simply rearranging those events, now saying that, in fact, a doctor had arrived miraculously in time to save Misery and her newborn baby.

But Annie is not fooled. In a remarkable scene, she strides into Paul's studio/cell, telling him matter-of-factly, "This is all wrong, you'll have to do it over again." In response to Paul's surprise, she launches into a story about her disappointment when, as a little girl, she realized that the "chapter-play" movie serials she loved to go see on weekends were in fact cheating on their plots—that while Rocket Man was left trapped in a burning car at the end of one episode, he was somehow able, without explanation, to escape from it at the start of the next. When Paul nervously agrees that "they always cheated like that in chapter-plays," Annie replies:

> But not you. Not with my Misery. Remember, Ian did ride for Dr. Cleary at the end of the last book, but his horse fell jumping that fence and Ian broke his shoulder and his ribs and lay there all night in the ditch so he never reached the doctor, so there couldn't have been any "experimental blood transfusion" that saved her life. Misery was buried in the ground at the end, Paul, so you'll have to start there. (1:01)

Like *The Shining* before it, King's *Misery* is a work of meta-fiction, a novel about writing a novel. But much of its self-reflexivity has a defensive edge. King knows it's only horror prose, but he likes it. In *Misery* he makes a case for the value of being a good writer of genre fiction rather than a mediocre author of serious literature. And what Paul learns from Annie is that to be a good popular novelist, he needs to respect his readers. He has to play fair, to observe the rules of the genre, and thus to start with Misery in the ground.

In the next scene Paul watches as Annie reads his revised opening. "Is it fair?" he asks. "Should I continue?" Annie gushes in reply, describing how, in this new draft, Paul has not only explained how Misery came to be buried alive (having lapsed into a coma resulting from a bee sting) but also used that plot twist to reveal a heretofore-unknown aspect of her character (her allergic reaction points to her descent from the aristocratic Lady Evelyn-Hyde) (1:02). The point is not that the new version is more realistic or artistic but that it now makes sense as the next book in the Misery series. Paul is playing by the rules he set up in his previous work. As Annie remarks later, "This is positively the best *Misery* you've ever written." Note: not the best *novel*, the best *Misery*.

I don't want to make too much of this lesson in genre, other than to stress that it *is* an actual lesson in genre. Paul learns something from Annie about his own practice as a writer, and the movie shows him applying that insight as he quickly composes the rest of the romance for her. In King's novel, it also becomes clear that Paul quietly agrees with Annie that "Misery's Return" is his best work in the series. To use the parlance of teaching writing, he begins to make the assignment "his own."

Nor do I mean to turn Annie Wilkes into some sort of model pedagogue. She is an ax murderer, a villain in a horror movie. But I think we can learn something about teaching by observing how she responds to Paul's writing. Perhaps I can clarify the point by contrast. In Todd Solondz's deeply unpleasant 2001 film, *Storytelling*, we are shown a college creative writing course taught by an imperious and self-absorbed professor. We witness two workshops in which the professor encourages his class to rip apart a story written by one of their classmates, and when they falter, he proceeds to eviscerate the authors himself. It's not that the professor's criticisms are wrong—from what we can tell, they seem on the mark. But his comments are unkind and unhelpful. "This is shit," he tells one young author. Uninterested in his students as either persons or writers, he has nothing to teach them. Annie Wilkes escalates the level of violence from the emotional to the physical—drugging, hobbling, and finally attempting to murder her one captive student. But she does, in her crazed and amateur way, value and respect Paul's work as a writer—and this puts her in a position to offer him a kind of advice the professor in *Storytelling*, despite his expertise, seems unable to offer his students. My point is that if we stop hoping that movie teachers will be versions of ourselves as we would most like to be seen, we might instead learn from watching what they actually do.

A DRAMA OF LANGUAGE

Let me close this chapter by returning closer to home. Earlier I mentioned that *Educating Rita* (1983) tells a familiar story of the reawakening of a middle-aged tutor, Frank, by a vivacious young student, Rita. But such a précis shortchanges the film and the play by Willy Russell it is based on. *Educating Rita* stands out among teaching movies for its interest in a student in her own right—rather than simply as a foil for her teacher. It is clearly Rita (Julie Walters) who, desperate to escape the confines of her working-class life, drives the action of this movie, pushing the languid Frank (Michael Caine) to teach her how to think and write about literature. The film discusses Rita's work as a writer no fewer than six different times, as she gradually learns to write the sort of critical essay needed to pass her exams. Most of these discussions take place in Frank's office, as he holds and points to the essays Rita has written. That is, the film keeps a consistent focus on the material labor of writing, on the actual production of pages and papers. (As well as on the work of reading them. We are shown Frank several times at his desk marking essays.)

The first essay Rita writes is, according to Frank, "all over the place." While it was supposed to be on E. M. Forester, it has more to say about Harold Robbins. When Rita protests that "you said to bring in other authors," Frank replies that "devouring pulp fiction is not being well-read" (19:00). He tells her she will need to become more disciplined and selective. But for a while, things only seem to get worse. Rita's second paper, in response to a prompt asking "how you would resolve the staging difficulties of Ibsen's *Peer Gynt*," consists of a single sentence: "Do it on the radio" (30:00).

When Frank protests that he might have "expected a considered essay," Rita explains that she needed to do her work for the course in the hairdresser's shop, and that was all she had the time to write. Frank sympathizes but insists on more. Rita takes her paper back and walks, with a mock goose-step, over to a table in his office, where she sits down to write while Frank grades other papers. In a few minutes she returns with this mini-essay, which Frank reads aloud:

> In attempting to resolve the staging difficulties in a production
> of Ibsen's *Peer Gynt* I would present it on the radio because as
> Ibsen himself says, he wrote it as a play for voices, never intend-
> ing it to go on in a theatre. If they had the radio in his day that's
> where he would have done it. (0:32)

Rita beams. Frank shrugs and nods. Rita has shown him that she
can translate her thoughts into the idiom of the academy and
that she can cite evidence from Ibsen himself for her proposed
staging of the play.

Of course, this moment of insight comes far too quickly and
easily. This is a movie, after all. But what I admire most about
Educating Rita is that it uses this deft and comic scene not as
a simple epiphany, marking the moment when Rita becomes
truly educated, but as the *start* of a long slog of learning. At her
next tutorial, Rita once again has no essay—but this time it is
because her husband, angry with what he sees as her betrayal
of their life together, has burned it along with her books. This
tension—between what Rita hopes to gain through her education and what she must give up to get it—is explored but not
resolved throughout the rest of the film. In a moving scene, Rita
speaks of her desire to learn how to "sing a better song," but the
film also pokes gentle fun at her fumbling attempts to speak in
an Oxbridge accent. Rita learns to give up that affectation but
grows more and more adept at writing critical prose. She writes
a paper that Frank describes as honest and affecting in its own
terms but not appropriate for an exam. Rita throws it into the
fire and starts over. Next she composes an essay that Frank tells
her "would not look out of place with these," gesturing toward
a stack of papers by full-time students. Rita is thrilled, though
Frank appears ambivalent. Finally, the two quarrel when Frank
accuses Rita of having abandoned her own voice in her quest to
sound more educated. But Rita *is* educated at this point, as she
angrily tells Frank and goes on to prove by passing her exams.
The movie ends with Rita and Frank reconciled but traveling in
different directions, neither quite sure what they will do next.

What strikes me through all of this is the unusual amount of
work we see Rita and Frank do together. We watch Rita writing

and revising, Frank commenting and grading, both of them conversing and quarrelling. The sets of the film are littered with books, papers, cigarettes, and coffee cups (which in Frank's case are usually filled with booze). No desks are leaped upon; no miracles occur. Early on, Frank describes himself as "an appalling teacher, which is fine for my appalling students"—and several scenes that portray him as drunk and supercilious in the classroom confirm this self-assessment. But Rita interests him and he takes her seriously. And so their relationship becomes, to return to Melora Wolff's phrase, a "drama of language"—that is, a drama of two people working together with texts and ideas.

The dead poets and wonder boys of the movies suggest that to teach writing we need to connect with the students we are working with. *Educating Rita* shows that doing so is not simply a matter of making friends. Rather, we need to approach and respect students *as writers*. We need to learn how to value what students have to tell us—indeed, to learn how to imagine them as people who may actually have something to tell us, something we can learn from, who are not merely our apprentices but our interlocutors. In chapter 2, I look at a few ways, some successful and others not, fictional teachers have tried to invite students into the conversations of the academy.

2

BEGINNINGS

I find it telling that one of the terms most often used to describe writing assignments is *prompt*. The word suggests that an assignment is something a student moves away from—and thus that the task of the teacher is simply to give their writing a nudge or a push, to get the ball rolling, the words flowing. This would seem to gainsay the idea that writing worth doing might have its roots in a set of questions, problems, ideas, or texts that students and teacher return to and think through *together*. You prompt an actor or politician to deliver a line or a singer or musician to perform a song. But you draw someone into a conversation, an exchange. As a teacher, I don't want to prompt students, I want to talk *with* them. It strikes me as a bleak irony, then, that we should describe the act of asking students what they think as a cue for them to perform, a prompt.

This is, of course, much what I have just argued in chapter 1—that the flaw of the dead poets and wonder boys as teachers is that they inspire and exhort but do not reply. Teaching writing involves more than assigning it. A good assignment needs to be more than a simple prompt. And yet . . . there is still the question of how to begin. In a celebrated 1985 essay, David Bartholomae suggests that a key task facing students as they enter college is one of "Inventing the University" as writers, of learning the distinctive moves and strategies of academic writing and making them their own. (Think of Rita as she revises her essay on staging Ibsen.) Bartholomae goes on to argue that the defining stance of the academic writer is oppositional, that these writers position themselves in some way against what is commonly thought or said. As teachers we thus need to find ways of helping students not to repeat what the culture has told

DOI: 10.7330/9781607329725.c002

them but to gain a critical distance from its maxims. This is an upbeat take on what many other commentators have noted less approvingly—namely, that academics often seem to use deliberately arcane language to set themselves apart from everyone else. But whether academic writing is seen as critical and oppositional or as obscure and elitist, the question remains of how you begin to make it your own.

That question is the focus of this chapter. How do students make the leap from one kind of writing to another? To find out, I look at four accounts of students trying to write their ways into the academy: David Mamet's 1993 *Oleanna*, Alan Bennett's 2006 *The History Boys*, Bel Kaufman's 1964 *Up the Down Staircase*, and Sapphire's 1996 *Push*. Bennett, Kaufman, and Sapphire offer hopeful stories of learning to write. *The History Boys* follows a group of suburban British schoolboys who must navigate the conflicts among their teachers as they prepare to write their university entrance exams. *Up the Down Staircase* shows a set of urban teenagers who slowly become more fluent as writers while their young teacher also struggles to find her own voice within a maze of bureaucratic demands and constraints. *Push* shows a young woman who, with the help of a remarkable teacher, battles horrific obstacles to learn how to write. In each of these works, new possibilities of writing are opened up. But in David Mamet's *Oleanna*, they are slammed shut. A student is silenced; a professor is impugned. Let me begin here by asking how that happens and what we can learn as teachers from Mamet's cautionary drama.

WHAT CAN THAT MEAN?

Oleanna dramatizes a teacher-student relationship as it careens from bad to awful. The play begins with an undergraduate student, Carol, sitting in the office of her professor, John, who is talking on the telephone. Carol has come to ask John about her grade in a course she is taking with him. She is doing poorly, perhaps failing, and repeatedly asks John to re-explain ideas and terms from his lectures. Self-absorbed and distracted, John often talks over Carol as she fumbles to speak and breaks off their conversation several times to answer the phone. Finally taking note of her increasing anxiety, John suggests a "deal" in which the two of them will start the course over, with Carol getting an automatic "A" on the condition that she comes to meet with him several times in his office (25). When this proposed deal fails to calm her, John tries to put his arm around Carol, who moves away from him. The first act ends with seemingly nothing resolved between them.

The second act begins with John asking Carol to withdraw a formal accusation of harassment she has made to his tenure committee. The two are once again in his office, but Carol has become far more composed. She now corrects John and refers to a mysterious "group" whose concerns she represents (51). When it becomes clear that their conversation is going nowhere, Carol tries to leave his office but is restrained by John. The act ends with her shouting at him to let her go.

The third and final act of the play shows John shamed and bedraggled. He has been dismissed from the university and lost his bid on a house. For the last several days, he has been sleeping in a hotel. Meeting with Carol for a last time in his office, he learns from her that when he does return home, he will face criminal charges for attempted rape. But now Carol offers *him* an "exchange" (72). If John agrees to have his own book removed from university reading lists, her group will withdraw its charges. Enraged, John attacks Carol, beating her and throwing her to the floor but stopping just at the point of rape, shouting "I wouldn't touch you with a ten-foot pole" (79). The play ends.

Oleanna was first produced in 1992 against the backdrop of the Clarence Thomas/Anita Hill hearings and campus debates over free speech and political correctness.[1] At that moment, it

---

1. A film version of the play appeared in 1994, directed by Mamet and featuring compelling performances by William H. Macy and Rebecca Pidgeon. Since then it has been revived often on the stages of college campuses and local theaters. For ease of citation, I refer to the published version of the play (Mamet 1993).

seemed clearly and almost exclusively a play about sexual politics, as critics and audiences debated over who was the real victim: John or Carol. This clearly remains an issue in the age of
#MeToo. But viewers have also begun to see the play as a par-
able about the politics of language and teaching.

This newer perspective improves the play. Mamet's take
on sexual politics is clumsy and exaggerated, as with each act
Oleanna falls deeper into melodrama. Carol's transformation
from an insecure student in the first act to a forceful accuser in
the second is implausible; her gnomic references to her "group"
are comically sinister. Meanwhile, John seems to be learning
how to speak like a man in a David Mamet play, shifting from
fastidious academic jargon at the start of the drama to shouted
expletives at its close. But however real his flaws as a teacher may
be, they do not merit the harshness of Carol's accusations. And
however exaggerated her charges may be, they do not justify his
assault. Mamet sets up his audience much as Carol appears to
set up John, seizing on a problematic exchange between a man
and a woman, a teacher and a student, as a pretext for airing a
set of grievances about gender politics.

But the actual setup is worth attending to. The first act of
Oleanna offers a close and nuanced study of a failed conversation between a student and her teacher. Carol and John simply
can't figure out how to talk to each other. Much of this problem
stems from John's unwillingness to take Carol seriously—as a
person and as a writer. Carol has come to John, she says, because
she feels baffled by the language of his course (6). But while
Carol actually pays very close, if at points perplexed, attention
to the language John uses, he shows almost no interest in her
attempts to speak or write—and in fact instructs her several
times *not* to write. He seems unable to imagine that she might
have something to say to him, and in failing to do so, he shuts
her out of the very discourse he claims to teach. A few moments
from the first act make this clear.

Oleanna begins with John speaking brusquely on the phone
as Carol sits waiting, unable not to listen in on his personal conversation, which is about the details of a closing bid he and his

wife are making on a house. The first words Carol speaks are to ask John about something she has just overheard him say: "What is a 'term of art'" (2). John replies with a tentative definition:

> It seems to mean a *term*, which has come, through its use, to mean something *more specific* than the words would, to someone *not acquainted* with them . . . indicate. (3, original emphases)

This seemingly random exchange is, of course, deliberate, as the rest of Mamet's play revolves around John and Carol's inability to understand each other; they are, as it were, speaking different languages, using different terms of art.

Carol picks up on this gap immediately, telling John that while she takes notes in class and tries to do "what I'm told," her problem is with "the *language*, the 'things' that you say" (6). When John dismisses her worries, patronizingly telling her she is "an incredibly bright girl" (7), Carol tries to explain that she comes a different socioeconomic class. But John barely allows her to get the words out. Instead, he picks up from his desk a paper Carol has written for him:

> Sit down. (*Reads from her paper.*) "I think that the ideas contained in this work express the author's feelings in a way that he intended, based on his results." What can that mean? (8)

This flip response drives much of what follows. True, Carol's sentence does not appear, on the face of it, to mean very much. She is struggling to write in a discourse she does not yet control. And all that she seems to have managed so far is to mimic something of the rhythm of academic prose, without yet being able to put those rhythms in service of an argument of her own. But still, John's condescension is astonishing. As a teacher, he makes no effort to learn what Carol might be trying to get at in that sentence or in the rest of her essay. Instead, he dismisses her language as meaningless and then tries to fill in that void with his own words.

And so, when Carol pleads with him to "*Teach* me. *Teach* me," John's response is to turn not to her work but to his own, asking her to point to moments in his book that she doesn't understand (11). This, predictably, leads nowhere. For Carol is still stuck on his scathing response to her paper. To say her writing has no meaning is to imply that she is stupid, she tells John. When he demurs, weakly, Carol insists that she actually agrees with him:

> No, you're right. "Oh, hell." I failed. Flunk me out of it. It's garbage. Everything I do. "The ideas contained in this work express the author's feelings." That's right. That's right. I know I'm stupid. I know what I am. (14)

Carol repeats almost these same words in the last lines of the play—at that point in response to John's calling her a "little *c**t*" (79): "Yes. That's right . . . yes. That's right" (80). The intellectual violence at the start of the play prefigures the sexual violence at its close.

At the risk of riding a hobbyhorse, though, I'd point out that at this still early moment in their conference, Carol has offered John yet one more chance to respond to her work. If he really doesn't think she's stupid, then what advice can he give her about revising her paper? But instead, John once again decides to talk about himself, launching into a meandering story about his own struggles to learn. This digression does not inspire so much as vex Carol, who eventually steers the conversation back to its starting point—her worries about her grade. And then John makes the egregious mistake of proposing his "deal":

> Your grade for the whole term is an "A." If you will come back and meet with me. A few more times. Your grade's an "A." Forget about the paper. You didn't like it, you didn't like writing it. It's not important. What's important is that I awake your interest, if I can, and that I answer your questions. Let's start over. (25–26)

It's hard to keep track of all the ways this proposal is a bad idea. It slights the intellectual work (whatever that may be) of John's course and field. It mocks any sense of fairness. It denies any obligations John may have as a professor to his school and its standards. It is flirtatious and possibly coercive.

It also tells the student to be silent. Carol is not to work at her writing anymore; rather, she is to stop writing. John is strict on this point. When, as they begin to "start over," Carol checks her notes, he instructs her not to (27–28). He restates this command a few moments later:

> JOHN: I spoke of it in class. Do you remember my example?
>
> CAROL: Justice.
>
> JOHN: Yes. Can you repeat it to me? *(She looks down at her notebook.)* Without your notes? I ask you as a favor to me, so that I can see if my idea was interesting. (29)

The job of the student is thus reduced to remembering and repeating. Indeed, John seems to suffer from what I'd call *xenographophobia*—a fear of the writing of others. John is proud of his own status as an author, eager to explain and add to what he has written in his book. But he will not discuss Carol's "meaningless" paper. He will not permit her to make notes, he constantly interrupts her, and he answers his own questions. And to some degree, his fears prove justified. It is through writing that Carol goes on to ruin him.

In the first act Carol asks John for instruction in writing but instead gets something more like a sexual pass—an embrace and a proposal that they continue to meet in his office. But the second act centers on a written text John is forced to respond to: Carol's complaint to his tenure committee. Threatened, John grows orotund. The act opens with him speaking at length about his love of teaching, his skills as a classroom performer, and his "covetous" pursuit of tenure (43–45). When he finally turns to the matter at hand, John begins, characteristically, by trying to evade what Carol has written:

> I know that you're upset. Just tell me. Literally. Literally: what wrong have I done you? (47)

Carol insists, however, that her answer is "in my report" (47), which John will thus need to read. And so he does, commenting in a professorial vein as he scans her text. His first response has a familiar ring:

> I find that I am sexist. That I am *elitist*. I'm not sure I know what that means, other than it's a derogatory word, meaning "bad." (47, original emphasis)

But now Carol denies his authority over her writing. She tells John that he no longer gets to decide what a word or text can mean or not.

> CAROL: We *do* say what we mean. And you say that "I don't understand you."
>
> /. . . . /
>
> JOHN: You see. You see. Can't you . . . You see what I'm saying? Can't you tell me in your own words?
>
> CAROL: Those are my own words. (49, original emphasis)

This is a powerful moment, if also a problematic one. John voices a suspicion shared in some way by many teachers—that while students may *speak* to us "in their own words," the texts they produce are somehow less reliable or authentic. Let me quickly say that I think this is a disastrous view for a teacher to take, that we need instead to assume that the texts students write are as much—or as little—their own as the words they speak. But I also suspect that John's xenographophobia is not uncommon among teachers. Students tend to be pliant and agreeable in person—as speakers and especially as listeners. It is tempting to think that when we talk with them in our classrooms or offices, they are presenting themselves to us as they really are. But the texts they write often seem intractable and maddeningly difficult to understand. How can it be that students who seem so bright and pleasant in person go on to produce papers that are so vague, flawed, and tendentious? Why don't they just tell us what they think in their own words? Or why don't we, as John proposes, simply dispense with writing altogether in favor of that welcome and easy sort of conversation that, as teachers, we are always routinely granted the pleasure of leading? Student writings disrupt our control over the smooth flow of talk in our classrooms. They force us to confront the thoughts and words of students in whatever unruly forms they may happen to take on the page rather than glide past them in conversation to the next comment or speaker.

And so, when Carol tells John that the words of her report *are* hers, she is insisting that he take her seriously as a writer, student, and person—that he respond to what she has to say. This moment would be more stirring, though, if it were clearer that she actually had written the report. For Carol has seemed to turn into an almost entirely different person in the second act of *Oleanna*. Where before she struggled to write a term paper for an undergraduate course, now she has evidently composed an articulate and damning report for a university tenure committee. And where before she seemed unsure about the meaning of familiar words like "hazing" (27), now she critiques John's "protected" and "elitist" use of the term (52). She mocks his "taste to play the Patriarch in his class" and lectures him on his use of a sexist phrase—"to overlook it is to countenance that method of thought" (51). In short, she is suddenly and scarily in charge. To underscore this transformation, several productions of *Oleanna*, including the 1994 film version directed by Mamet, have Carol change from her undergraduate uniform of jeans and shirt in the first act into a kind of business suit in the second.

How do we explain this dramatic change in personality? One possibility is that Carol has been playing a deep game all along—that she entraps John in the first act with a pose of girlish insecurity as part of a deliberate plan to expose and shame him. But such a calculated scheme seems farfetched and unmotivated. What I find more plausible is that in seeking some way to explain what happened in John's office, Carol has somehow stumbled upon her mysterious "group"—"the people I've been talking to" (54). This group seems to offer her two things that John does not—a sense of being listened to and a language to use in understanding her situation.

Unfortunately, this language—at least as Carol deploys it—proves as clichéd as John's academic jargon. Throughout the second and third acts, Carol often seems to be reciting phrases she has just been taught—"paternal prerogative," "protected hierarchy," "a sexist tinge," "removed from inclusion as a representative example of the university." In repeating such shopworn phrases, she does not invent the university so much as ventriloquize one of its discourses. We hear her group speaking through her.

It seems reasonable to guess, then, that the group has also helped Carol write her report. And indeed, in the third act, Carol refers repeatedly to the list and statement she presents for John's signature as something "we" have produced (71–73). She is thus twice denied a voice as a writer over the course of the play. John shows no interest in what she has to say, and the group exploits her as a mouthpiece. Near the end of the play, Carol shouts that what she wants is not revenge but "understanding" (71). Once again the *–ing* form is important. For Carol no longer wants, as she did in the first act, simply to understand John. She now wants to reach an understanding *with* him, to be heard and understood by him. But this never happens.

Mamet shows little empathy for Carol as a person. On the contrary, over the course of his play she becomes ever more a caricature—an aspiring academic feminazi in a business suit. Still, though, he draws a clear portrait of her vulnerability as a student, of her position outside of discourses that John and her group control. This power of teachers to accept or exclude has been seen as the real tension driving the play by several critics who read *Oleanna* as commenting on the aggression that lies just beneath the surface of much university teaching. For what can really be learned in a conversation whose unstated goal is to reaffirm the authority of one speaker over the other?

Drama scholar Lee Papa offers a quirky and revealing take on this problem in teaching in his 2004 article "Mamet's *Oleanna* in Context." Trying to help students in an Intro to Theater course see how John uses his authority as a professor to intimidate Carol, Papa stages a classroom reading of several scenes from *Oleanna*. What is peculiar, though, is that Papa decides to play John himself while asking a student he identifies as the "teacher's pet" to take on the role of Carol. Not surprisingly, almost everyone in the class is made uncomfortable by this arrangement—especially Jenn, the young woman asked to act the role of Carol, who was required to rehearse scenes, in a disturbing mimicry of the action of the play, alone with her professor in his office. Papa is sensitive enough to realize that he overstepped boundaries with this exercise, but he also argues that it had two positive effects.

Students who had until then seen John simply as the victim of a calculated setup, he tells us, now began to see how he is also a kind of intellectual bully. And Papa (2004, 228) himself began to recognize "the exploitative and exhibitionistic qualities of the performance—exploiting Jenn by asking her to rehearse this, exploiting the students by asking them to view it." Ironically, much like John, the character whose flaws he aimed to demonstrate, Papa's eagerness to be the star of his own classroom makes him deaf to the anxieties of his students. His article thus shows, perhaps more than he had hoped, how hard it can be to alter the power dynamics between teacher and student.

I think one way we might change those dynamics is through writing. When student texts are taken seriously, when a teacher becomes not only a lecturer of students but a reader of their work, when "what can this mean?" is heard not as a dismissal but as a question calling for response, then a new relationship between student and teacher becomes possible. The insight of *Oleanna* lies in its repeated suggestion that the conversation between John and Carol could have gone otherwise, that they might have talked with rather than struggled against each other. Among all the other questions it raises, then, the play poses an urgent, practical problem in teaching: How can we help students like Carol write their way into the university? This is a question taken up in its most literal form by Alan Bennett in his 2006 play *The History Boys*, which centers on a group of British schoolboys preparing to take the entrance exams to Oxford and Cambridge.

THOUGHTFUL OR SMART?

The History Boys contrasts three styles of teaching. The play is set in the 1980s in a second- or third-rank private school in the north of England.[2] But while the school may be undistin-

---

2. *The History Boys* premiered in London in 2004 and was made into a film in 2006. Both play and film were directed by Nicholas Hytner. The film features extraordinary performances by Richard Griffiths, Stephen Cambell Moore, and Frances de la Tour. For ease of citation, I refer to Bennett's 2006 print version of the play.

guished, its headmaster is ambitious. He has decided that several of his sixth-formers (all boys) should apply to Oxford or Cambridge and has hired a young consultant, Mr. Irwin, to coach them for their exams in history. Irwin joins Mrs. Lintott, a teach-the-facts historian, and Mr. Griffiths, an English master who teaches anything else but—his classes filled with appreciative discussions of poetry and reenactments of old movie scenes. Irwin's expertise is exam writing. He's there to show the history boys how to write essays that, if nothing else, "will not be dull"—that will grab the attention of the "bored examiner" who has just read "a hundred and sixty papers each more competent than the last" (19).

Facts, feeling, cleverness. The play centers on the tensions among these values in teaching—and ends up suggesting that a real education involves all three. While the headmaster of the school is portrayed as a comic figure, an overweening bureaucrat, he has somehow engineered a situation in which the history boys can learn far more from observing the differences among their three teachers than they might otherwise learn from any one of them. And so they do, with all eight in the end passing their exams and several winning scholarships. A weakness of the play, it seems to me, lies in its depiction of the students—a group of rather-too-charming English schoolboys who run to type: the jock, the Romeo, the sensitive kid, the fat kid, the smart kid, the minority, and so on. But the three teachers—Lintott, Hector, and Irwin—emerge more fully as individuals. We see their strengths and failings, in the classroom and in person, as well as the commitments and anxieties that drive their teaching. Through them *The History Boys* pictures what it might mean to be perhaps not a heroic teacher but still a pretty good one.

Much of that teaching centers on writing. The history boys are stuck as writers at a stage of knowledge telling but not knowledge making—their essays show that they've mastered the required readings but not that they have anything of their own to say. Hector has had them learn poems and movie scenes by heart; Lintott has drilled them in the facts of history. But they haven't learned how to mobilize what they've learned, to make what they know part of an interesting and lively argument of their own. As Irwin remarks about an early set of their papers:

> So we arrive eventually at the less-than-startling discovery that so far as the poets are concerned, the First World War gets the thumbs-down. (23)

In response, though, Irwin has only a single gimmick to offer the boys as writers: the unexpected reversal. As he argues about the World War I poets:

> If you read what they actually say as distinct from what they write, most of them seem to have enjoyed the war. Siegfried Sassoon was a good officer. Saint Wilfred Owen couldn't wait to get back to his company. Both of them surprisingly bloodthirsty. (25–26)

Hector disparages this sort of ready contrarianism as a tactic of mere "journalism" (72). He worries that Irwin is teaching the boys simply how to make points rather than how to figure out what they might actually think or believe. The play proves him right on both counts. We learn that Irwin later goes on to become a pundit on BBC history programs, and here is how one of the students summarizes his approach to writing:

> Find a proposition, invert it, then look around for proofs. That was the technique and it was as formal in its way as the disciplines of the medieval schoolmen. (35)

What Irwin thus has to teach is a method of invention, a way into the arguments of the academy. As he puts it, "A question has a front door and a back door. Go in the back, or better still, the side" (35.) Almost alone among teachers portrayed in fiction, Irwin proposes a technique for writing that is something other than "just tell the truth"—which is the only actual advice his rival Hector has to offer the boys (83). For Irwin, writing history is "not a matter of conviction" but of finding an "angle" on a question (33). The great strength of this technique is that it can be used to support almost any position. But that is, of course, also its weakness. As the play goes on, we learn that Irwin has much to hide. He is drawn sexually to one of the boys, and he did not attend Cambridge as he claims. Much of what he has to offer is thus a pose, a way of playing the game without ever fully showing your hand.

But Hector's approach is also flawed. The first act of the play ends with a moving scene in which he and a student talk about a poem by Thomas Hardy (53–57). The student has memorized "Drummer Hodge" and recites it beautifully. But it is Hector, not the student, who comments on the meaning of the lines, noting that even though the young soldier Hodge is thrown in an "uncoffined" grave, he is not left anonymous; his name is still recalled for us by Hardy. Hector is, at that moment, wondering how he will be remembered. He has just been told by the headmaster that he must resign his position at the end of term, having finally been caught at his long-standing practice of lightly fondling the students in his charge. The boys seem to view his advances with amusement—perhaps because he is old and fat and thus, they assume, beyond having sex. And Bennett, I must say, also seems less worried by Hector's behavior than one might hope—more inclined to view it as indiscreet rather than abusive. But while his gropings clearly diminish Hector as a person, they also hint at what drives his pedagogy. Like so many other teachers, Hector aims to seduce his students intellectually, to make them into versions of himself, to have them take on his tastes and passions. As a result, they leave his classes having soaked up his views more than having formed their own.

This problem is made clear through an ongoing wager Hector has with the boys. They reenact some of the flotsam of popular culture and he tries to identify it. So long as the boys aim for what seems to them the obscure—Gracie Fields, the closing scenes of *Brief Encounter* and *Now, Voyager*—Hector wins and they must pay up. But he is finally stumped, near the end of the play, when one of the boys sings a pop song that is actually popular at the moment, the Pep Shop Boys' 1987 "It's a Sin." While one of the other students protests that "you can't expect him to know that . . . and anyway it's crap," Hector is more gracious or resigned and concedes the game: "his crap or my crap, it makes no difference" (104). But that seems to me precisely the problem. If Irwin has only technique to offer students, Hector has only crap—snippets, touchstones, quotations.

The History Boys ends with Hector telling his students to "pass the parcel . . . That's the game I wanted you to learn. Pass it on" (109). But it's a particular sort of parcel that Hector seems to have in mind, less something his students might make or write than something they've learned, memorized, had handed to them by someone else. It is revealing that his fiercest criticism of Irwin is to call him a writer, a journalist. Indeed, like John in *Oleanna*, Hector seems adverse to having students write. Instead, he has them memorize and recite poems, songs, and movie scenes. When one complains that he doesn't understand poetry, Hector replies, "Learn it now, know it now, and you'll understand it whenever" (30). But when Irwin suggests that the boys actually put such "gobbetts" of literature to use in their exams, Hector takes violent exception:

> Oh it would be useful . . . every answer a Christmas tree hung with the appropriate gobbets. Except that they're learned *by heart*. And that is where they belong and like the other components of the heart not to be defiled by being trotted out to order. (48, original emphasis)

What Hector has to teach is meant to be valued for its own sake. As one of the boys patiently explains to Irwin:

> Mr. Hector's stuff's not meant for the exam, sir. It's to make us more rounded human beings. (38)

But however rounding or improving it may be, the sort of learning Hector has to offer is also inert—since to use it would be to betray it, turn it into gobbetts.

And so, if Irwin's pedagogy may lead to cynicism, Hector's risks ending in silence. We see this dilemma unfold in a brilliant scene in the second act of the play, when the two teachers try to lead a class discussion together. The students are at first uncertain how to behave:

HECTOR: Come along, boys. Don't sulk.

DAKIN: We don't know who we are, sir. Your class or Mr. Irwin's.

IRWIN: Does it matter?

TIMMS: Oh yes, sir. It depends if you want us thoughtful. Or smart. (70)

The rest of the scene shows that they need to be both. At Irwin's suggestion, they begin to talk about how to formulate a response to an exam question about the Holocaust. Hector objects:

> HECTOR: How can the boys scribble down an answer however well put that doesn't demean the suffering involved? And putting it well demeans it as much as putting it badly.
>
> IRWIN: It's a question of tone, surely. Tact.
>
> HECTOR: Not tact. Decorum.
>
> LOCKWOOD: What if you were to write that this was so far beyond one's experience silence is the only proper response.
>
> DAKIN: That would be your answer to lots of questions, though, wouldn't it, sir?
>
> HECTOR: Yes. Yes, Dakin, it would. (71)

If Irwin's attitude is glib, Hector's is defeated. While Irwin pushes the students to find a "perspective" on the Holocaust that moves them past the "stock answer" condemning it (73–74), the only possible response Hector can imagine is outrage. Each of them, of course, is right, in his own way. Irwin is right to tell the boys that doing history depends on gaining a critical distance from your subject; Hector is right to see the violence involved in turning the Holocaust into just another subject to write on. The question is how to join Irwin's detachment with Hector's passion. A good writer must somehow find a critical perspective on a subject without losing his investment in it.

The History Boys leaves this as a problem in writing that the students must solve for themselves. Neither Irwin nor Hector has the capacity to solve it for them. The play hints that Irwin possesses real talent as a writer, as he goes on to be a successful journalist. But he is nervous and brittle, over-aggressive, as a teacher—reducing intellectual work to a simple "habit of contradiction" (44). Hector is warmer and wiser as a person, despite his pawing of the boys, but Bennett goes out of his way to spell out his limitations as a teacher in a scene in which his colleague and friend, Lintott, correctly accuses him of substituting the "consoling myth" of art for the hard work of education. "Or what's all this learning by heart for," she says, "except as some sort of insurance against the boys' ultimate failure" (69).

Lintott is the only woman with speaking lines in the play, and she does not directly compete with Irwin and Hector for the allegiance of the history boys. She is the teacher who has gotten them this far, who has trained them to pass their A-level exams, but who has, in her own words, little else to offer them but "more of the same" (8)—the same being a continued drill in the facts of history. She represents what the boys are trying to move beyond. In a nice irony, though, she is also the person who hints most clearly at how they might fuse Irwin's technique with Hector's sensibility. In a scene near the end of the play in which the three teachers are conducting mock interviews with the students, Lintott is provoked to complain how "dispiriting" it has been for her, as a woman, "to teach five centuries of masculine ineptitude" (83–85). What Lintott reveals in her brief and unexpected polemic is a passionate investment not in getting ahead on exams or in quoting poetry or films but in her actual work, her subject: history. Her outburst is met with an embarrassed silence, which is quickly covered over with the sort of schoolboy banter that makes up most of the play. No one in the room, including Hector and Irwin, is ready to hear what she has to say.

As Steve Benton notes in his fine 2008 dissertation "Ichabod's Children," what makes *The History Boys* stand out as a drama about teaching is that it lacks an idealized teacher as its protagonist. Irwin, Hector, and Lintott are all good teachers who are serious about their work—but Bennett makes their limitations very clear: Irwin is too clever by half; Hector, poorly disciplined; Linttot, dull. But taken together, they offer the history boys—and the audience of the play—a glimpse of what a compelling education might be: provocative, invested, and well-grounded.

By inference, that is also the play's view of good academic writing. But inference is all we have. For as much as *The History*

Boys talks about writing, it shows us none. We know that the students pass their exams, but Bennett is more interested in what their teachers have to tell them about writing than in what they might actually write. That is a familiar and unfortunate flaw in books and plays about teaching. By way of contrast, let's look at a text that shows a remarkable interest in the writing both students and teachers do: Bel Kaufman's 1964 novel, *Up the Down Staircase*.

JETSAM

Robert Mulligan's 1967 film version of *Up the Down Staircase* is a remarkable, gritty depiction of teaching in an urban public school. Shot in East Harlem in a semi-documentary style, with many students played by non-actors, the film follows the struggles of a first-year teacher, Sylvia Barrett, portrayed with an unkempt intensity by Sandy Dennis, as she confronts both an underachieving class of eleventh graders and an indifferent public school bureaucracy. For the most part, the film follows what I've called the dead poets narrative—as Sylvia slowly connects with students, forms allies with sympathetic teachers, and learns to live with the obduracies of the administration. But the student she cares about most eludes her, the colleague she thinks might be a beau proves instead a cad, and a girl she might have helped injures herself leaping from a window in a moment of lovesick adolescent folly. In the end, Sylvia does not triumph so much as endure. Offered the chance to transfer to a swank suburban private school, she opts to return for a second term teaching in Harlem.

And yet, as powerful as this film is, it actually obscures what is most striking about the novel on which it is based: Bel Kaufman's 1964 *Up the Down Staircase*. For while Mulligan's film follows a coherent narrative arc, Kaufman's novel is fragmented, diffuse, epistolary. While the movie centers solidly on Sylvia Barrett, the novel continually spins out and away from her, consisting almost entirely of quotidian and often anonymous texts—memos, notes, forms, circulars, minutes, flyers, news articles, homework, suggestion box comments—produced by students, teachers, and administrators over the course of a term. (The novel had its beginnings as a short story Kaufman published in 1962 in the *Saturday Review*, titled "From a Teacher's Wastebasket.") More than any other book I've ever read, *Up the Down Staircase* represents a class as a collective project, an amalgamation of voices—students, teacher, librarian, school psychologist, department chair, vice principal, and others.

Several story lines emerge out of this jumble of texts: Sylvia grows more confident in meeting the needs of her students and the demands of her superiors; she starts but then backs away from a romance with a colleague; she tries but fails to connect with a smart but disaffected student. While Sylvia narrates parts of these stories in letters to friends and notes to fellow teachers, we need to construct most of them from scraps written by students and memos posted by administrators. Indeed, the key incident in the novel does not directly involve Sylvia. Kaufman reproduces the notebook of Alice Blake, a girl in Sylvia's homeroom who has formed a crush on her English teacher, the handsome and urbane Paul Barringer, a poet manqué who is teaching high school "while waiting to be published" (58). (He is also the colleague Sylvia nearly falls for.) We read along as Alice uses her notebook to compose drafts of a love letter to Barringer, speculates on his possible romance with Sylvia, and practices signing her new married name ("Alice Barringer")— all of this interspersed with homework for French, English, and math. The notebook ends with a copy of a handwritten letter Alice finally works up the courage to leave on Barringer's desk, in which she declares how she alone among her classmates feels "the Beauty and the Truth of the poetry you read" and offering "if you ever need me to die for you I gladly will" (232). In a moment of stunning cruelty, Barringer corrects a number of mistakes in spelling, clichés, and punctuation in her prose and returns her heartfelt if naive letter to Alice. (We are shown his corrections penned in the margins of Alice's letter.) Devastated, Alice decides that like the Lady of Shalott (one of Barringer's favorite poems), she will kill herself for love. Fortunately, she only breaks a few bones in a leap from a second-story classroom window, as we learn in the next chapter though a series of frantic memoranda from administrators managing the incident.

Sylvia shares a love of reading with Barringer and admires his easy wit and poise. But this incident reveals him to be everything she wants not to become as a teacher. As she writes to a friend: "Paul asks how *I* would have handled a love letter from a student. I don't know—by talking, maybe, by listening. I don't know" (240, original emphasis). And indeed, listening rather than correcting turns out to describe her best work as a teacher. Looking for ways to engage her class of "slow non-readers," Sylvia starts a suggestion box and we read the entries—some signed and some pseudonymous—at three points during the novel. A few are heartbreaking—an anonymous student ("Me") wishes himself a happy birthday, since no one else knows—and many others are irreverent and funny: "You're a good teacher except for the rotten books you have to assign like The Oddissy. I wouldn't give it to a dog to read" (113). The main thing is that they keep coming—even from "The Hawk," whose comments all end with some version of "from now on I'm not writing any more for you" (76)—and by the end of the semester, most of the entries are signed. (The Hawk turns out to be Lennie Neumark, a boy embarrassed by having fallen out of his seat on the first day of class.) A sense of trust and respect is achieved. Sylvia also asks students to comment anonymously on what they learned in English during their first two years in high school and gets a series of ungrammatical but astute critiques. For example, "Dribs & Drabs. McBeth one week Moby Dick next, a quotation mark, and oral debates on Should Parents be Strict? Should Girls Wear Jeans" (81). And there is a remarkable chapter, "From Miss Barrett's Wastebasket" (92–105), in which we read the "scrap paper" drafts of student essays tossed among Sylvia's own (and equally unsuccessful) attempts to begin a letter applying for a new job.

The point, made over and over and in ways too comic, astute, and varied for me to summarize here, is that there is a difference between being smart and being educated. John gestures toward this distinction in *Oleanna* when he assures the failing Carol that "you're an incredibly bright girl" (7), but he clearly doesn't believe it. But *Up the Down Staircase* documents Sylvia's real and growing appreciation of the intelligence of her charges. Indeed, she begins to see how her eagerness to instruct can impede her efforts to understand. This is illustrated in a hilarious account of a class discussion of *Macbeth* in which Sylvia's students continually ignore her attempts to correct their speech:

> I: I understand Macbeth was taught in English 2 last term. You were supposed to report on a supplementary book. That means, in addition to the required—
>
> LOU: I ain't never read it before.
>
> I: I never read it.
>
> LOU: Me neither.
>
> / . . . . /
>
> I: Rusty, you wanted to say something?
>
> RUSTY: Mrs. Macbeth noodges him.
>
> I: You mean nudges?
>
> RUSTY: Noodges. Being a female, she spurns him on. (191–93)

Here Lou shows the timing of a borsch-belt comedian, and Rusty is right twice-over: Lady Macbeth *is* a noodge, and her egging on of her husband combines a disdain and ambition that are precisely caught in *spurn*. As Sylvia learns to listen, her students grow more confident in what they have to say and write. She teaches through offering them her attention.

We don't often see Sylvia respond to student writing, though, and her one sustained effort to do so marks perhaps her biggest failure as a teacher. Sylvia is immediately drawn to an outsider in her class, Joe Ferone, a tough kid who seems in almost constant trouble with the vice principal and other teachers. When Joe writes a dismissive response to her question about what he's learned in prior English classes ("You teachers are all alike dishing out crap and expecting us to eat it"), Sylvia responds with a kind of forced interest, praising his "vivid" writing but noting "though your vocabulary is colorful, certain words would be more effective if used sparingly." Joe's response is "I don't understand them big words you use" (82–83). Undaunted,

Sylvia continues to push for Joe, defending him against accusations of cheating, excusing class cuts and other misdemeanors, and even giving him a second chance when he brings a knife to school. However, Joe misunderstands the nature of her interest and, in a tense scene, makes a rough pass at Sylvia when the two of them are alone in a classroom. When Sylvia tells him no, gently, he bolts from the room, possibly crying, and is pretty much lost to her as a student for the rest of the semester (300–303).

Sylvia fails with Joe Ferone because she is drawn not to who he is but to who she would like him to be. "I dimly sense a rebelliousness in him, like mine" (59), she says. She begins by over-praising his writing, much as she starts by over-admiring the supercilious Paul Barringer. Neither boy nor man quite turns out to be the sensitive rebel she hopes for. In contrast, one of Sylvia's triumphs comes when she asks Jose Rodriguez—who we learn was the quiet boy who wished himself a happy birthday in the suggestion box—to serve as the judge in a classroom mock trial (136–37). Jose brings an unexpected authority to the role—drawing on his own experiences in juvenile court to keep strict order over his classmates, as though he had simply been waiting all that time for the right occasion to speak. Later, he writes to Sylvia in the suggestion box that "ever since you elected me judge . . . You made me feel real" (180).

My complaint about most dead poet movies has been that they glamorize the work of teachers, of inspiring and assigning, but show much less interest in the work of students. This emphasis is turned on its head in *Up the Down Staircase*. Sylvia's assignments and lessons are actually pretty routine: "Why do we study myths?" "What are your views on integration?" and so on. The energy of the novel comes less from her than from the comic, intelligent, and unpredictable responses of her students.

INCUNABULA

Still, *Up the Down Staircase* offers little sense of what a teacher might do besides listen. How might we actually prod students to develop their beginning attempts at writing? Sapphire offers some striking examples of a teacher doing so in her 1996 novel *Push*.[3] The characters in *Push* make the streetwise kids in *Staircase* look like the prep schoolers in *The History Boys*. Set in 1987, the novel centers on Precious Jones, an illiterate sixteen-year-old girl living in Harlem with her termagant mother and carrying a second child by her father. Hopelessly behind in her conventional high school, Precious transfers to an alternative class in basic reading and writing, a pre-GED course. *Push* tracks her growth as a writer despite horrific obstacles: racism, incest, abuse, homelessness, HIV.

The person who sets that growth in motion is Miss Blue Rain, the confident and perceptive teacher of the pre-GED course. At the very start of their work together, Miss Rain asks Precious to read the first page of a children's book, "A Day at the Shore." Precious confides to her what she has until then managed to conceal from the rest of her teachers: "The pages look alike to me" (53). In a remarkable scene, Miss Rain doesn't judge Precious but also doesn't excuse her from the task, first telling her to "look at the page and say the words you do know," next to use the illustrations as clues to other words, and finally to sound out, with her help, those that remain. Using this mix of guesswork and decoding, Precious slowly constructs the words "A Day at the Beach." Not perfect but a start, as Miss Rain clearly feels:

> She closes the book and says very good. I want to cry. I want to laugh. I want to hug kiss Miz Rain. She make me feel good. I never readed nuffin' before. (54–55)

Miss Rain's strategy is essentially to teach reading through writing. She tells her class of six young women that they must write in a journal for fifteen minutes each day. When one of them asks her "*How* we gonna write . . . if we can't spell?" she replies, "push yourself to see the letters you're thinking" (60–61). Much of the novel shows Precious struggling to do just

---

3. Sapphire is the pen name of Ramona Lofton, a New York City performance artist, writer, and teacher. *Push* was her first novel. In 2009 Lee Daniels produced and directed a film version that, while faithful to the novel, spends less time documenting the growth of Precious as a reader and writer than it does the horrors of her abuse.

that. Her first entry is "li Mg o mi m." Miss Rain translates these attempts at sentences—in this case writing "Little Mongo on my mind" (61)—underneath the words Precious has written in her journal. But she also responds to the content of what Precious has to say—asking her for more information or to explain a thought or sometimes to challenge her thinking. For instance, after Precious gives birth to her second baby, a social worker at the hospital suggests that she might consider putting him up for adoption. But Precious writes in her journal that her grandmother has told her that "onle dog drop babe an wak off (*only a dog will drop a baby and walk off*)." Miss Rain writes back:

> Dear Precious,
>
> Don't forget to put the year, '88, on your journal entries.
>
> Precious you are not a dog. You are a wonderful young woman who is trying to make something of her life. I have some questions for you:
>
> 1. Where was your grandmother when your father was abusing you?
> 2. Where is Little Mongo now?
> 3. What is going to be the best thing for you in this situation?
>
> Ms Rain (71)

There is so much going on in this brief response, all of it admirable. In reminding her to date her entry, Miss Rain is asking Precious to be serious and careful about her work as a student and writer. She then quickly declares her unreserved support for Precious as someone "trying to make something of her life." And her concluding questions push Precious in two important ways—both by asking her to question her grandmother's right to tell her what she ought to do and by subtly encouraging her to write more. Precious decides to keep her baby, but she also begins to put her reasons for doing so into writing: "I is be bt met cdls ed" (*I is best able to meet my child's need*) (72). Her teacher doesn't persuade her of a plan of action but rather engages her in a process of reflection.

In many ways, Blue Rain is like Sylvia Barrett as a teacher. Both respect the good will and intelligence of their students. Neither confuses a mastery of writing with an active mind. But as the title of Sapphire's novel suggests, Blue Rain is far more willing to *push*. She is the teacher as midwife, coaxing what is inside Precious and her classmates out onto the page. Perhaps the most moving moment in the novel comes after Precious tells her classmates she has learned that, as a result of her ongoing abuse by her father, she is HIV positive. Blue Rain suggests that the students write in the journals and, for the first time, Precious refuses. She feels defeated, drowned. Miss Rain insists; Precious lashes out at her, cursing, screaming that she doesn't know what she has been through:

> Class look shock. I fell embarrass, stupid; sit down, I'm made a fool of myself on top of everything else. "Open your notebook Precious." "I'm tired," I says. She says, "I know you are but you can't stop now Precious, you gotta push." And I do. (97)

Blue Rain is one of the most remarkable teachers in literature. But she is only a supporting character in *Push*. Precious is its hero. The novel is written in her voice, and the frequent entries from her journal document her growing fluency as a writer. As time goes by, Miss Rain needs to translate less and less for Precious, as her spelling improves and she begins to write in full if erratically formed sentences. She discovers a flair for image-based poems and starts to read books like *The Color Purple* (whose structure in some ways resembles that of *Push*). All of this takes time. *Push* ends with a set of stories and poems in a class book, "Life Stories," compiled in 1991, four years after Precious first begins to study with Blue Rain. This book shows that Precious has still not quite caught up with her classmates as a writer. She is represented by three short poems in a book that extends over thirty pages. In the last of those poems, though, Precious refers to Langston Hughes, Louis Farrakhan, Alice Walker, and her teacher, Miss Rain, suggesting that she is not simply putting words on paper but imagining herself as a writer among writers.

The point, it seems to me, is that the accomplishments of a teacher are best shown not through classroom brilliancies, speeches from the top of a desk, but in the writing of students. In 2009 Lee Daniels directed *Precious*, a strong film version of *Push,* with powerful performances by Gabourney Sidibe as Precious and Mo'Nique as her mother. But the movie suffers from the same problems as the film version of *Up the Down Staircase.* A drama of language is subsumed by a narrative of personal growth. Unable to render the writing of Precious and her classmates, Daniels's film offers uplift in the place of intellectual development. As portrayed by Sidibe, Precious seems a remarkable and endurant young woman, but the role writing plays in her life and education is, at best, only hinted at.

In *Oleanna,* John is unable to listen to Carol, and her "group" uses her as a mouthpiece. In *The History Boys,* neither Hector nor Irwin is able to offer their students more than a version of themselves, but, thrown together as co-teachers, they willy-nilly offer the boys a new set of choices in writing. In *Up the Down Staircase,* Sylvia Barrett does listen, and as a result her students write to her with increasing confidence and fluency. But it is only in *Push* that we see a teacher, Miss Blue Rain, who both respects the intelligence of her students and also insists that they attempt something more, something beyond what they now feel capable of doing. In chapter 3, I turn to several more examples of teachers working with student texts and of students working with the comments of their teachers to see how it is that a text might be written by one person and yet, somehow, also depend on the thoughtful responses of another.

3
WORK IN PROGRESS

In my reading I've come across only one fictional writing teacher who seems at all aware of the field of composition. Unfortunately, he is also a terrible teacher, compulsive gambler, kvetch, and would-be womanizer. Pack Schmidt is a middle-aged nobody professor of English in *Mustang Sally* (1992), a bleak campus spoof by Edward Allen. Describing his coursework near the start of the novel, Pack offers quick nods to process, freewriting, and *Writing with a Purpose*. But if he knows a little bit about best practices in composition, it is probably because he is no longer allowed to teach much of anything else. Both his life and his career are washouts—divorced, lonely, bored, stuck at an obscure midwestern university, more interested in gazing at the sorority girls who take his intermediate composition courses for an easy grade than in teaching them anything about writing. And so, when Pack refers to meeting "the writing authority Donald Murray" (160), it is a detail that further places him as part of a small and unimportant professional world, much as, in another sort of campus novel, a quick allusion to chatting with Stanley Fish or Edward Said or Paul DeMan would establish the speaker as a member of a globe-trotting academic elite. As Pack himself says:

> For the level of my own classes, none of the theoretical stuff matters much. I don't need to learn about Foucault . . . and I probably won't get thirsty enough to attend the Marxist cash bar following the symposium about new ways of incorporating Race-Class-Gender into remedial composition classes. (86)

And so once more, comp equals mediocrity.

In a series of plot twists both elaborate and familiar, *Mustang Sally* offers Pack redemption through sex. He falls head over

DOI: 10.7330/9781607329725.c003

heels for Mustang Sally, a beautiful former student who is now a sex worker in a Nevada brothel, and lurches with her through a series of escapades both on and off campus, beginning, as he does, to imagine an alternative to the dreariness of his current life. It's a classic wonder boy narrative and a somewhat tired academic farce. What intrigues me, though, is a long passage early on in the novel (30–37), when Allen reproduces in full the final paper, "Things Happen in Pairs of Three," Sally writes for Pack's class in intermediate composition. Like Chaucer's Tale of Melibee, the point of this extended seven-page quotation appears to be to prove just how bad a writer Sally is—as well as how uninterested Pack is in her work. Sally appends a note to her essay, apologizing that "it's not very good, but I have been so busy that I didn't have any more time to revise it like you always want people to" (36–37). Pack agrees, thinking to himself after he reads her aimless series of anecdotes:

> There was a time when I would have given this paper the F it deserves, but then I would have gently guided the student through the long revision process, which would have brought it up to a C-minus or so, and everybody would have been happy. The problem is that it's just so much work. (37)

Instead, Pack just cuts to the chase—offering Sally a series of innocuous comments and meaningless edits and giving her paper, "despite its first-draft feel" (37), the C-minus he figures it would eventually get anyway.

Mustang Sally is an unappealing novel. Like Mamet's *Oleanna*, it is a diatribe against the perceived excesses of the sexual politics of the early 1990s, but unlike Mamet's conflicted play, it is strident and boorish in its voicing of male grievance. However, it does offer a painfully accurate example of how the teaching of writing can so often go wrong. Sally just fills up space on the page. Pack's assignment asks her to "come up with a personal theory about some aspect of reality, and to use as many specific examples to show how that theory operates in real life" (30). The paper she writes in response, "Things Happen in Pairs of Three," echoes the thoughtlessness of the assignment. In turn, Pack fills up much of the white space remaining on the page with his own red-inked marginal notes "about run-on, frag, awk, what?, sp, confusing" (37). But neither of them much cares—who would?—about whether things actually happen in pairs of threes or not. As Sally puts it, laughing, after reading Pack's comments:

> You should have given me an F . . . I was drunk and it was the middle of the night. You don't have any standards at all, do you? (61)

Sally and Pack thus tacitly agree to have a non-conversation, a mock intellectual transaction that seems uncomfortably similar to the sex for money that begins the next phase of their relationship. It's all work for hire. She pretends to have something to say; he feigns interest; a grade gets assigned.

But there are other scenes in fiction that show teachers and students talking together about writing in very different ways—that depict conversations with a use value as well as an exchange value. I think it's worth looking at such scenes to see what might help a teacher and student move beyond the sort of formulaic transaction Sally and Pack are caught within. How can we talk with students in ways that actually help them rethink and improve their writing?

To get at some answers to that question, I look in this chapter at several novels whose plots center around the work teachers and students do together in a writing course: Jincy Willet's *The Writing Class* (2008), William Coles Jr.'s *The Plural I* (1978) and *Seeing through Writing* (1988), and Alison Lurie's *Love and Friendship* (1962). I then turn to two novels that depict an older writer mentoring a younger one: Antonio Skármeta's *The Postman* (1985/1995) and Pat Barker's *Regeneration* (1992). None of these books offers a simple plan for responding to writing, but each suggests ways a teacher can guide the work of beginning writers without wresting control of it from them. Before I turn to these hopeful accounts of teaching, though, I need to consider the more troubling view that to really learn to write, a student must first be willing to submit—in both mind and body—to a master artist and teacher.

WRITING, TEACHING, AND SEX

Part of the lore of graduate school is that brilliance allows for, perhaps even requires, a certain level of arrogance, impatience, and assertion. One way of proving you're no fool is to show that you do not suffer them gladly. To this day, the figure perdures of the eminent professor—uncompromising, exact, passionately devoted to their discipline, their craft, loathe to share its secrets with all but the most talented students. In many plays and stories about writing, this eminent professor also possesses an unerring ear for an original voice amid the babble of workshop strivers and acolytes. That is why students sign up for their courses, in the hope of being heard, of being recognized as a real writer.

For instance, in her brief novel *All Is Forgotten, Nothing Is Lost* (2010), Lan Samantha Chang tells the story of Roman Morris, a talented young poet enrolled in an MFA program somewhere in the Midwest. Roman is drawn to Miranda Sturgiss, the star of the writing faculty, who is so ruthless, aloof, and dismissive as a teacher that students refer to her classes as "bludgeonings" (12). Yet they line up to take her courses in the hope that her acumen as a critic and prestige as a poet will somehow help them advance in their careers.

The ambitious Roman launches into a secret affair with the somewhat older Miranda, whose husband is in England. He tapes a note on his desk saying "*all that matters is the work*" (26, original emphasis). He desires Miranda more as a muse than a lover, going to her "almost every night, bringing drafts and pieces of his work" (29). And yet the odd thing is that the novel never shows us any of Roman's work. We are left to assume that it is good for much the same reason he does—because Miranda says it is. Genius recognizes genius. But although we are told that Miranda "was as critical a reader as she had ever been, insisting upon revisions and then questioning every word of them" (58–59), we are never shown any of the poems Roman is writing and revising and that her questions are said to spur forward. Rather, the work the two of them do with his writing is kept hidden, an intimacy like sex and perhaps connected to it.

As the novel progresses, Roman leaves Miranda and becomes a successful poet and teacher in his own right. In a striking scene, set near the present, Roman reflects on the differences between his and Miranda's approaches to teaching. At this point in the novel, Roman is himself middle-aged and working with a talented young undergraduate, Veronica, who is writing a novel based on her struggles with anorexia. One afternoon Veronica shows up in his office in tears and it occurs to Roman, as he consoles her, that in some earlier time (say, the 1980s), he might well have had an affair with her. Nowadays, of course, such relationships are frowned upon. Roman's feelings are mixed:

> He did not know if the rules were most helpful in preventing a student from suffering abuse or in avoiding a situation where the other students watched jealously from the outside, knowing they were learning relatively little, while one of them had an access to so much. (148–49)

Here the links among teaching, writing, and sex are made explicit. The best-case scenario is one in which a teacher bestows their attention on a favorite, a beloved. Having once been so adored, Roman is ready to grant the connection between the intimacies of sex and learning. After all, he thinks, what has replaced it? According to Roman, students now

> believed that writing could be "taught" by the dissemination of "craft," and that anyone with the smallest speck of ability or desire was entitled to the dissemination. No one bludgeoned anybody anymore. (146–47)

So what does Roman do as a teacher, in this new age, with Veronica? It seems much like what Miranda did with him when they were not having sex—he offers a close line-by-line reading of her work in a series of "two-hour bouts" that leave him "wrung out" from the effort (147). But over the course of all these editorial bouts, we are offered little sense of what sort of comments are being made on what kind of manuscript. We are simply told that a promising writer has met an experienced reader and asked to imagine the strenuous and passionately charged intellectual work they do together.

It fascinates and irks me that a novel centered around the teaching of writing has so little to say about it. Chang is the director of the celebrated Iowa Writers' Workshop, and her descriptions of the vanities, intrigues, and anxieties of the world of academic creative writing are spot-on. But what happens on an *intellectual* level between Roman and Miranda, and Roman and Veronica, remains mysterious. It's as though writing exists in two parallel worlds—a visible one of social networking and professional infighting and another, hidden one of ineffable craft.

If that is true, then it makes sense in two ways to sleep with your professor, since in doing so you can both make connections to get ahead in your career *and* receive the direct ministrations of genius. This seems the takeaway lesson of Theresa Rebeck's literary sex romp, *Seminar* (2012).[1] Rebeck's play is a lighthearted send-up of the pretensions of both aspiring writers and their teachers. Its main character, Leonard, is yet another failed novelist, now a journalist, editor, and egomaniacal cad who trades on his inside ties to the world of publishing to offer a series of private and very expensive seminars to promising young writers. The four students in his current seminar are Douglas, an author of shallow yet finely drawn short fiction; Izzy, an enterprising hottie who will write or do anything to get ahead; Kate, an Upper West Side intellectual whose stories are studied reworkings of Jane Austen; and Martin, an earnest type who believes in Art. It is, in short, a setup for farce, which is what Rebeck delivers. Each scene in the play is a new meeting of the seminar: Leonard stops dead at the first semicolon in Kate's rewriting of *Pride and Prejudice*, professes to love Izzy's two pages of soft-core porn and beds her after class, finds Douglas "not without talent" and suggests that he try Hollywood. The students complain among themselves about his arrogance and compete for his attention. Scene after scene is dead-on and funny.

---

1. *Seminar* premiered on Broadway in 2011. I regret not having seen it, since the lead character of Leonard was played first by Alan Rickman and then by Jeff Goldblum. My analysis is based on my reading of Rebeck's 2012 print version of the play.

But *Seminar* also subscribes to the same myth of genius—and its connection to sex—as *All Is Forgotten, Nothing Is Lost*. Leonard introduces Izzy to Salman Rushdie and Douglas to Harvey Weinstein (a detail which perhaps resonates differently now than when Rebeck was writing). After some handwringing, Kate decides to sleep with Leonard. and gets a ghostwriting gig as a result. Martin is the holdout. In the last scene of the play, he goes to Leonard's apartment to demand a refund, only to discover that Leonard has not only read his manuscript but, recognizing its worth, edited its first section:

> LEONARD: I finally read those pages that idiot Bob Gladeau sent me. The first twenty pages of your masterpiece. I did a line edit for you, show you what you got.
>
> . . . *Martin sits, and reads.*
>
> MARTIN: So you think I . . .
>
> LEONARD: You're just hearing too many words.
>
> . . . *Martin continues to read. After a moment he looks up.*
>
> MARTIN: This is—fantastic.
>
> LEONARD: It really is the only way to learn anything about writing, to have a decent editor go through it word by word for you. Help you see what it is, what you meant. What you didn't even know you meant. (102–3)

This is the real romance. Martin and Leonard don't sleep together, but in an outburst that fuses sex and writing, Leonard offers to be Martin's editor, promising him:

> LEONARD: I will fuck you up in so many different ways you won't even know who you are anymore. That seminar was the prelude . . . How serious are you? You want to be a writer or not? (104)

So Martin has found his soul mate, his editor, the person who hears his voice. But what is that voice? What is Martin writing about? What changes has Leonard made? We never learn. We simply look on as the two bond in some sort of mystical artistic communion.

Both *All Is Forgotten* and *Seminar* set up a dialectic between bludgeoning and intimacy. The fierce critic in seminar becomes the selfless reader in private—willing to invest hours refining the work of a single, talented student they have chosen from among the rest. Both also imagine the work of teaching writing as almost exclusively editorial in nature. Neither Miranda nor Leonard helps their charges *develop* the projects they are writing; rather, they are both shown working line by line, sentence by sentence, on the drafts of their students, "questioning every word." Good writing is pictured as hinging on the turn of a phrase and good teaching as involving a lover's attentiveness to detail.

It may be that you can only learn some things about writing from such close and intimate work with a master. I don't know. I've never done it. But if that is indeed the case, *All Is Forgotten* and *Seminar* fail to show us what those things are. Miranda tells Roman that their affair is part of his "poetic education" (77), but we never see how she influences the poetry he writes. Leonard promises to "fuck Martin up" into being a real writer, but again, we never actually see the work he does on Martin's manuscript. We are left instead like the students Roman describes as watching from the outside, excluded from the secrets whispered by their teacher to a favored pet or protégé. The transfer of genius, it seems, always takes place in another room, behind closed doors.

WORKSHOPS

So it is with relief and pleasure that I turn to a set of books that show some of the actual work of teaching writing. Jincy Willet's *The Writing Class* (2008) is a murder mystery set in a university adult extension course in fiction writing. The workshop is taught by Amy Gallup, who is, you will not be surprised to learn, a failed novelist. She is also, however, a talented and enthusiastic, if at times irritable, teacher of writing. There are twelve students in Amy's class, one of whom, embittered by countless rejections from publishers, begins to anonymously terrorize the others—first with scurrilous unsigned reviews of their writing, then with a series of increasingly violent pranks that culminate, inevitably, in murder. In the mode of *Ten Little Indians*, Amy and the remaining students must figure out which one of them is the killer before he or she strikes again.

The Writing Class does not strive for profundity, but it does offer a smart and witty take on several issues in writing—particularly on how we respond to the voice or self a writer projects on the page. For the main clues Amy and her class have to the identity of the killer come from the short pieces of fiction each of them has written, as well as the comments they've made about each other's work. And this proves a not very reliable set of clues. As the discussion in Amy's classes reveals, what many of these beginning writers construct is a kind of idealized version of themselves—who they would be if a movie star was acting them. And so, for instance, the doctor in the class, who clearly views himself as superior to the rest of the students, writes a thriller with an annoyingly virile physician as its lead character, while the middle-aged matron writes a fantasy of domestic revenge in which a wronged wife kills her indifferent spouse. Others fail to get past the clichés of the genres they are writing in—populating their stories with vampires and private eyes whose personalities are drawn more from pop culture than from life. And the stories that are good—an older woman preoccupied with the infidelities of a young neighbor, a day in the life of a high school geek—conceal their authors through their art. This uncertain relationship between the real-life author of a piece and the voice we hear speaking in it is illustrated midway through the novel, when on Halloween evening, as a lark, Amy's students all show up for class wearing costumes, confounding her attempts to call the roll and playfully evoking the concept of *persona*—the idea that a writer constructs a mask through which to speak.

One of the things I like most about *The Writing Class* is that no one it, including Amy, is shown to have unsuspected reserves of talent. Most of the characters in the novel are passable writers, a few are pretty good. I do think we see them learn about writing, but less through what they write than through how they learn to talk about one another's work in progress. At each of their meetings, the class discusses stories written by two different students. There are six of these workshops over the course of the novel, so we get to see at least a paragraph or two from the writing of each of the twelve students. (It's a well-plotted book.) The first workshop gets off to a rocky start when a student reads a poem about a failed suicide. Some members of the class rush to assure her that everything will be okay, that she is among friends, while others look uncomfortable at having unexpectedly found themselves in a "group therapy situation" (28). Amy's response is helpfully brusque. She insists that everyone in the class has the "absolute right to have his manuscript assessed *as fiction,* and each reader has the solemn duty to read it that way" (29, original emphasis). From that point on, her course (at least before it gets sidetracked into a search for a murderer) becomes a practicum in doing just that: discussing not the content but the craft of a piece of fiction.

In the first few workshops, Amy plays a strong role in both starting and redirecting the conversation about a piece. She's quick to push beyond the compulsive attempts of one student to praise just about anything that anyone writes, especially for their "use of metaphor" (147), as well as the equally predictable complaints of another student about the sexual politics of almost every story they read. She insists on certain rules for discussion—insisting that readers summarize what a story is about before either criticizing or applauding it and quickly silencing authors when they try to break into the conversation about their stories. She explains literary techniques as needed. In short, she does not hesitate to act the professor—and new teachers of writing would do well to study the moves she makes as a leader of class discussion.

By about the fourth class, though, the students start doing much of this work for Amy. They've grown more at ease with one another and more willing to separate their responses to a piece from their feelings about its author. There's no clear turning point, as there rarely is in an actual course. But students begin more and more to talk to each other rather than respond to questions Amy asks them. For instance, there's a remarkable scene midway through the novel when a young woman, Tiffany, whose piece is about to be discussed, gets cold feet and disavows her story before the class has a chance to talk about it. One of her classmates gets annoyed, insisting that he wants to discuss the story because, it turns out, he is impressed by how Tiffany draws her readers immediately into the mind of her narrator. Another student agrees with him that the voice of Tiffany's narrator is compelling but notes that almost nothing happens in the story. Amy then looks on as the members of the class

> wrangled for fifteen minutes over whether Maggie had an epiphany (she hadn't), and for another ten over whether "Untitled" was really a story at all or a vignette, and Amy didn't need to distinguish between the two because Carla did so neatly, from memory . . . Edna offered measured praise for the piece's linguistic cleverness, Chuck and Frank backed her up, and the slackers—Harry, Marv, Syl—whom Amy could usually count on to say nothing unless they liked a story, complained that if nothing happens, it isn't finished. (155–56)

And so on. What I find striking here is that not only does Amy drop out of this debate but, in a way, so does Tiffany. That is, the conversation of the class is no longer focused simply on offering her advice but rather on figuring out what everyone in the room might learn as a writer from reading her story. Of course, that is a remarkable complement to pay any writer, and Tiffany realizes as much. As the class draws to a close, she apologizes for "pretending that this piece didn't matter . . . thanks for taking it so seriously" (156).

You'll recall that Amy's class is also being stalked by an anonymous killer. At their final meeting the members of the writing class reread together the emails, parodies, and story reviews the anonymous killer has sent to each of them, seeing if they can figure out the person hiding behind the prose. They can't. But in an odd way, that proves reassuring. For in rereading, they find a critical angle on texts that had previously terrified them. Looking at the killer's clever, self-consciously erudite phrasings, they start to sense someone desperately eager to show off. One student, not the best writer in the class, remarks that he tried to write a few sentences in the style of the killer to see what it would feel like and quickly gave up: "This is the way people write when they want to make you feel stupid" (284). A teacher to the end, Amy gushes:

> "What you just did is what I've been trying to get you to do all semester—read with your own eyes, listen with your own ears. That was a genuine critical response to the reading, Syl." (284)

The others agree with Syl. While the killer is adept at writing in a wide range of voices, which is what makes it so difficult to figure out who she or he might be, all of those voices seem calculated, above all else, to impress. And, ironically, as soon as a reader catches on to that strategy of intimidation, it ceases to work. The author now seems to bluster more than threaten.

The killer is eventually revealed through other means. *The Writing Class* is not a novel of literary detection in which the identity of a criminal is revealed through their words. If anything, it is something closer to the opposite—a novel that explores the gaps between the self on the page and in everyday life. It's also a lot of fun. Amy has been through a couple of marriages, publishers, jobs, careers—all of which has left her skeptical and droll but not jaundiced. As the novel progresses, she really begins to like the members of her class, more for who they are as persons than for what they might become as writers. So do we. The novel thus suggests several ways of tracking the progress of a writing class. One involves students doing more of the work of the class and the teacher less, another with a move away from simple advice giving and toward considering the possibilities and questions raised by a piece, and still another with the class becoming a group people simply like being part of, whose conversations they enjoy and value.

A MEAN SOCRATIC METHOD

But these are not necessarily the goals of every writing teacher. For instance, in *The Plural I* (1978), William Coles describes a class that seems quite deliberately no fun at all. Coles is an unusual figure in that he was not so much a novelist who taught composition (there are plenty of those) but a composition teacher who wrote novelized accounts of his courses. *The Plural I* is a detailed, class-by-class account of a required writing course Coles taught in the late 1960s at Case Western Reserve University. Coles required his students—all science majors, all men—to write a short essay for each of the thirty meetings of the course. He tells us that he has reproduced the assignments and student essays featured in the book exactly as they were written; the rest is, in his words, a "novelistic account of teaching and learning" (4). Each of the thirty chapters dramatizes a class meeting. Each of those classes focuses on a couple of student papers written in response to the latest assignment Coles has given. The assignments are sequenced to prod students to think in increasingly complex ways about what it means to be a professional or an amateur. The student essays are always discussed anonymously, even though their authors are sitting in the room. And so each chapter of the book shows us Coles aggressively leading his class in a conversation about the work they are all doing right then and there as writers.

The Plural I is the work of a curmudgeon. Coles constantly scolds and harangues his students, upbraiding them to pay closer attention to the particularities of the essays they are discussing (and writing). He is flatly not interested, as he says early on, in "Making Friends" (34). Rather, he wants students to give up a game he feels they have all learned to play only too well in school, in which the point of writing is to be clear and correct and to please the teacher, and instead to write in a way that expresses something of who they actually are, of their own voice or style. For Coles, though, forming a style is less a matter of letting go, of freeing yourself up, than of resisting influence and convention. Originality results from struggle. Like Roman in *All Is Forgotten*, Coles is suspicious of reducing writing to technique; unlike Roman, he believes most of us are capable, if pushed, of doing something more.

And push is exactly what Coles does, over and over. His encounters with students in *The Plural I* are true bludgeonings. Here, for instance, is an exchange from early in the term. The class has just read a student essay defending the role of the amateur in a world of professionals. It's a competent yet vapid piece, the kind of thing that could be written by almost anybody. Coles begins by asking students to comment on the voice they hear in the writing:

> No one, of course, had any idea of what I was talking about.
> "I think he proves his point pretty well here."
> "Yep," I said. "No question. It's well-organized. It's Clear, Logical, and Coherent. It's neat. Is that what you mean?"
> "Well, yes."
> "OK. But could we let that kind of talk ride for a minute? Would you mind taking up the question of who's talking in the paper?"
> He just looked at me.
> "Or isn't that part of the game?" I said.
> "I don't know what you mean."
> "I didn't cross you up, did I? I didn't get out of the mold with all that business about voice? You know, the English Teacher mold?"
> "I'm not sure . . ."
> "Look. Read the first two sentences of the first paragraph out loud. Just read them out loud."
> He did.
> "'It is somewhat irrational,'" I said. "How much is 'somewhat,' would you say?"
> "I guess he could be a little more concrete there."
> "'A little more concrete.' My God. Look, how old do you think the writer of those two sentences is pretending to be?"
> "How old?"
> "Well how big then? Do you think he's really the size of the Jolly Green Giant?" (21)

The conversation goes on, with Coles continuing to badger his students to admit what he is convinced they can all already see—that this writer, like almost everyone else in the class, was simply writing to fill up the page, to get the assignment over and done with, and thus that his voice, to the degree that he has one, is an attempt to sound smart without really doing much thinking. Coles will have none of that. Class after class, he hectors and cajoles students to distinguish between the glib and the thoughtful.

In the class meetings that follow, Coles offers praise sparingly but not begrudgingly. A good sentence or two over the span of an essay is noted as an achievement. The quality of the student writing improves, and even more, so does the quality of their discussion. Notice how, in the conversation I've just quoted, Coles leaps on the tentative comment of a student in the class—"'A little more concrete.' My God"—with a vehemence equal to his criticisms of the anonymous essay they are discussing. That sort of battering diminishes as the term goes on and as students learn to read for the unexpected, self-reflective phrasings Coles values as a sign of individual voice.

The Plural I is a hard book to categorize. Coles was a teacher of college composition, and his book is addressed to fellow comp teachers. (He was one of my senior colleagues when I taught at the University of Pittsburgh in the 1990s.) He speaks in his own voice throughout and claims to be working with documents written by actual students. But his aims seem less scholarly than novelistic. He does not, that is, try to present data about teaching collected in any sort of rigorous manner or to argue for a certain theory of writing. Rather, as he puts it, he is interested in "the actual doing, on how a given theory of rhetoric or approach to the teaching of writing feels as an action" (3). Like a novelist, he hopes to offer insight, not fact. It thus seems to me that The Plural I is best read as fiction—as an attempt to evoke the lived experience of a certain kind of intellectual work.

In The Plural I, that work takes place not in the library or at a typewriter but in the classroom. It shows Coles actively thinking through a set of texts with students, not simply presenting information to them. And it suggests the extraordinary level of effort and focus involved in returning, class after class, paper after paper, to the question of how a particular writer creates, or fails to create, a sense of their own voice on the page. Coles drives his students relentlessly and works himself even harder. Exertion serves as proof of caring, of seriousness. The Plural I offers the best sustained account of teaching as intellectual work that I know of. It is also clearly a book written by an obsessive. The Plural I doesn't make me want to teach like Coles. But it does suggest what it would feel like to bring his kind of intensity, rigor, and creativity to the writing classroom.

The weakness of *The Plural I* has to do with its portrayal of students. There's no question about Coles's commitment to his students as writers; he quotes and analyzes dozens of their texts. But we're never offered backstories for any of the students, and all of their essays are discussed anonymously. In addition, Coles rarely identifies the other speakers in class by name, and much of the dialogue in the novel has a wooden feel. So we are left trapped, as it were, inside Coles's head, his version of the class.

I suspect that Coles himself felt this as a limit, since in a later book, *Seeing through Writing* (1988), he essentially reverses this emphasis. *Seeing through Writing* is clearly fictional—although its aims are also more plainly didactic than those of *The Plural I*. (Coles intended the book to be used in college composition courses.) The novel tracks the efforts of several students to respond to a sequence of assignments (only twelve this time) exploring the question of what it means to really "see" something. Ironically, the author of this sequence, a teacher nicknamed the Gorgon, is never directly seen or heard from except in the words of his assignments and in remarks repeated and puzzled over by his students. And in sharp contrast to *The Plural I*, the novel does not include a single classroom scene. Instead, each chapter depicts students at work outside of class on the assignments set for them by the Gorgon—drafting, revising, outlining, note taking, arguing, procrastinating, pondering, responding to each other's writing. They are shown in study groups, pairs, and alone. And they all have histories or at least pocket bios—the math whiz, the mom returning to school after years spent raising kids, the addict in recovery, the college girl who still loves *The Wizard of Oz*, and so on. But the narrative thread of the novel soon becomes hard to follow, as the focus of each chapter shifts unpredictably from one student to the next. And on top of that, the book is visually over-complicated—using several typefaces to set off the Gorgon's assignments, excerpts of published works, typed student essays, and footnotes from the main text of the novel and then adding to that mix of fonts still more reproductions of handwritten essays, notes, and comments on papers.

I admire the experiment, but in the end this layering of texts fails to make up for a set of earnest and flat characters. The Gorgon remains by far the most interesting figure in the novel, perhaps because everyone else in it spends so much of their time trying to interpret the aims of his labyrinthine assignments and the meanings of his cryptic utterances. And I suspect that *Seeing through Writing* might have been a more interesting novel if it didn't try to be a textbook at the same time. (The idea was that actual students would also write in response to the Gorgon's assignments and compare their efforts with those of the characters.) Still, Coles's work remains an unusual and intriguing attempt to use fiction to teach academic writing.

Alison Lurie's deft and moving first novel, *Love and Friendship* (1962), offers a cautionary backdrop for reading Coles. *Love and Friendship* tells the story of Emily, a young woman slowly falling out of love with her husband, Holman, an instructor of writing at Convers College. Holman is part of the teaching staff of Humanities C, a course that is clearly based on English 1–2 at Amherst College, where Coles taught for several years at the start of his career. Headed for decades by a legendary taskmaster, Theodore Baird, English 1–2 influenced the work of many noted teachers of writing. Its structure provided the template for the course in *The Plural I*—students wrote for every class meeting, responding to a series of questions centering on problems of definition. (The terms and concepts at the center of the class changed each year.) In *Love and Friendship*, Emily describes the course as "conducted by a kind of mean Socratic method" (18), in which teachers refuse to provide answers to any of the questions they pose, on the theory that students will only learn how to write through formulating those answers on their own.

But this is not to say that the questions allow for a range of responses. Rather, as Emily puts it:

> "The meaning of this word (or line) depends on the other words (or lines) which surround it at the time I use it," was the basic answer to the current set of questions, but the students had to find this out for themselves, and nobody was allowed to tell them. (18)

Bright but jobless and bored, Emily asks Holman to share the assignments he writes for Humanities C with her in the evening as they have drinks together, and she tries to figure out what the desired response would be. The result is that the two slip into an unfortunate parody of classroom talk, with each statement Emily makes met by a question from her husband:

> "Well, but. Oh, I see. If you want to put it that way. Is that what I'm supposed to say? That the photograph is a kind of map?"
> "What do you mean by a 'kind of map'?" (20)

This is, of course, no way for two adults to talk with each other. The more Holman retreats into the peculiar discourse of Humanities C, the more Emily draws away from him. The rest of the novel explores the consequences of this widening emotional gap between them with considerable insight and finesse.

Love and Friendship suggests that when taken outside the classroom, the habits of talk promulgated by courses like Humanities C may actually become destructive. (This is also the thrust of *Wit*, Margaret Edson's fine 1999 play about a literary scholar facing terminal cancer.) The sort of course described with skepticism by Lurie and with enthusiasm by Coles proceeds with a calculated aggression. The classroom becomes a kind of surgery, as old ways of thinking and writing are rooted out so new ones can take their place. There is no move to make the classroom a space of equals; the teacher is always several steps ahead. The appeal of this approach lies in its intellectual rigor and sense of mission, and for those reasons I was much drawn to Coles when I first started teaching. But the mode of address throughout his writing is always that of master to disciple. He thus has little to suggest about how people might talk together as equals about writing.

TEACHING AS MENTORING

Such a conversation does not need to be a collaboration or even an exchange between writers of equal skill. But I do think you can teach writing without taking on the pose of sage or guru or taskmaster—that is, without talking *down* to students. You can instead approach students as something more like a fellow writer, a co-worker. Let me close this chapter with two examples of such conversations among peers.

In her great novel about World War I, *Regeneration* (1992), Pat Barker imagines a series of conversations between two soldier poets, Wilfred Owen and Siegfried Sassoon, while both were convalescing in a sanatorium in Scotland. The younger and at the time lesser-known of the pair, Owen, has been charged with editing an in-house literary journal, *The Hydra*, as part of his treatment for shell shock. He tentatively approaches the more distinguished Sassoon for a poem. Sassoon agrees to contribute but also asks to read some of Owen's work.

One of the first poems Owen brings to him imitates the style of Sassoon's own war poetry. But Sassoon is not much taken by the complement, insisting instead that

> the *fact* that you admire somebody very much doesn't mean they're a good model. I mean, I admire Wilde, but if I started trying to be witty and elegant and incisive, I'd probably fall flat on my face. (124, original emphasis)

Owen gets the point—he and Sassoon are very different sorts of writers—but still wants to work with the older poet. Sassoon, in turn, sees that the young man clearly has talent and, taking on the role of mentor, puts Owen on a strict writing schedule: "It's like drill. You don't wait until you feel like doing it" (125).

In response, Owen begins to draft what will become one of the most harrowing poems ever written about war. He brings an early version to Sassoon, leading to this extraordinary exchange between them:

> Sassoon took the sheet and read the whole poem through twice, and then returned to the first two lines.
>
> > *What minute-bells for those who die so fast?*
> > *—Only the monstrous/solemn anger of our guns.*
>
> "I thought 'passing' bells," Owen said.
> "Hm. Though if you lose 'minute' you realize how weak 'fast' is. Only the monstrous anger . . ."

"'Solemn'?"

"'Only the solemn anger of our guns.' Owen, for God's sake, this is War Office propaganda.'"

"No, it's not."

"Read that line."

Owen read. "Well, it certainly isn't meant to be."

"I suppose what you've got to decide is who are 'these'? The British dead? Because if they're *British*, then 'our guns' is . . ."

Owen shook his head. "All the dead."

"Let's start there." Sassoon crossed out *our* and penciled in *the*. "You're sure that's what you want? It isn't a minor change."

"No, I know. If it's 'the,' it's got to be 'monstrous.'"

> *What passing-bells for those who die . . . so fast?*
> *—Only the monstrous anger of the guns.*

"Well, there's nothing wrong with the second line."

"'In herds'?"

"Better."

They worked on the poem for half an hour. (141–42, original emphases)

While this conversation is fictional, it is based on actual events. Sassoon and Owen did indeed meet in 1917 while both were recuperating at Craiglockhart War Hospital in Edinburgh, Scotland, *The Hydra* was a real journal, and the changes Barker has Sassoon suggest to Owen do in fact appear, in Sassoon's handwriting, on an early draft of Owen's famous antiwar poem, then titled "Anthem for Dead Youth." (A digitized image of this draft with Sassoon's comments can be found on the British Library website.) What Barker does in her novel, then, is dramatize the process of revision by creating a scene that lets us eavesdrop on a writer and teacher as they work together on a text.

That work is, of course, far more incisive than most of us can hope to imitate. Owen and Sassoon focus tightly on a set of word choices—*minute-bells* or *passing-bells*, *solemn* or *monstrous*, *our guns* or *the guns*. But each of those choices has a kind of ripple effect. One change leads to the next. As Owen remarks, "If it's 'the,' it's got to be 'monstrous.'" The changes they discuss are thus not mere editorial corrections, simple substitutions of one word for another, but revisions that affect the stance and meaning of the poem as a whole.

Such work with texts is the meat and potatoes of teaching writing. We spend much of our time trying to help writers think through the implications of using one word or the other, or crafting a sentence in this way or that, or striking a certain stance or tone, or starting or finishing their essay on a particular note. So you might think our scholarly literature would be filled with nonfictional versions of Barker's imagined conversation between Owen and Sassoon.

It is not. I suspect one reason it is not is that we have been preoccupied with, as it were, Sassoon's side of the conversation. Since the 1980s, scholars in composition have argued for a mode of responding to work in progress in which teachers help students develop their projects as writers rather than simply correct their prose. That is excellent advice. But there has been surprisingly little work done on the *uses* students make of teacher comments. There has been little attempt, that is, to track changes, to chart the actual work students do from draft to draft. Instead, the focus of researchers has been directed predominantly on what the teacher, not the student, has to say. The effect is to suggest that teachers can decide on a style of response in advance of commenting on any particular essay—that our comments are driven not by what students have to say to us but by what we have already decided to tell them about writing.

In contrast, Barker is interested not simply in what Sassoon has to say to Owen but in the not entirely predictable uses Owen makes of his advice. Some days after the conversation I've quoted, Owen returns to Sassoon with yet another version of his poem. When Sassoon asks him what draft this is, Owen replies that he's lost count, that, after all, Sassoon did tell him to "sweat his guts out." Sassoon replies:

> "Did I really? What an inelegant expression. 'What passing-bells for those who die as cattle?' I see we got to the slaughterhouse in the end." Sassoon read through the poem. When he'd finished, he didn't immediately comment.
> "It's better, isn't it?"

"Better? It's *transformed.*" He read it again. (1992, 157, original emphasis)

But after offering this silent testimony to the power of what Owen has written, Sassoon goes on to argue some more with the direction the poem has taken, worrying that Owen might offer his readers a false sense of consolation for the meaningless slaughter of the war. But Owen objects to this reading of his work, insisting that one can take "pride in the sacrifice" without suggesting it was justified. Indeed, Owen points out, Sassoon makes a similar move in one of his own poems about the war, which Owen begins to read triumphantly to his teacher (157). Sassoon cedes the point to his newly confident student but still makes one last and telling revision, changing *Dead* to *Doomed* in the poem's title (158).

What matters most to me is not how this conversation ends but that it *is* a conversation, an exchange in which both writer and reader, student and teacher, assert their views about the text they are working on. Barker shows us a process in which both Owen and Sassoon win, lose, and compromise—and through which a better text is forged. The poem remains Owen's, but Sassoon has had a hand in its shaping. It is a remarkable depiction of the kind of work with writing a student and teacher can do together.

TEACHING AS FRIENDSHIP

Barker's aim in *Regeneration* is to explore the psychic effects of war on different sorts of men, and Owen and Sassoon are but two of many characters in the novel. So her insights into writing and its teaching form only a small part of her larger purpose as a novelist. In contrast, Antonio Skármeta's *The Postman* (1985/1995) centers on the relationship between an older writer and his protégé.[2] Most of the events of the novel occur

---

2. Skármeta first published his novel in Spanish in 1985 as *Ardiente Pacienca,* or *Burning Patience.* The book became well-known to readers in English as *The Postman* only after the release of the 1995 film, *Il Postino,* directed by Michael Radford. The movie was a clear labor of love by its lead actor,

between 1970 and 1973. Its protagonist is Mario Jiménez, the young postman of Isla Negra, a remote fishing village on Chile's southern coastline. Mario has only one customer on his route, the renowned poet Pablo Neruda. Mario asks Neruda for his help in winning the heart (and loins) of the beautiful Beatriz, a barmaid in the village. Not very reluctantly, Neruda agrees, giving Mario copies of his poems and explaining how metaphors function in them. Mario seduces Beatriz with metaphors borrowed from Neruda. Smiles stretch across her face like butterflies, her laugh is a sudden silvery wave, and so on. Mario also begins to carry around a notebook in which to compose his own poems and metaphors, although it never becomes clear just how much writing he actually does in it.

Mario's new interests in poetry also involve him in politics. Neruda briefly runs for the presidency of Chile before withdrawing in support of the Marxist Salvador Allende. His friend Mario thus becomes known not only as an aspiring poet but a socialist. This has tragic consequences at the end of the novel when bloody reprisals follow Allende's overthrow by a right-wing coup.

The Postman is filled with Neruda's poetry. Mario is a kind of literary magpie, picking out bright images and metaphors from Neruda's verse for his own use. When he begins to court Beatriz, he speaks to her "first with vehemence and then as if he were a puppet and Neruda the ventriloquist," soon gaining "such fluency that images flowed out of him magically" (35). This has led some readers to criticize the politics of the novel, arguing that it never allows Mario to form his own voice.

But Neruda is not simply a Cyrano; he is also a teacher and friend. And Mario does form a voice of his own. This becomes clear midway through the novel when Neruda is called away from Isla Negra to serve as Allende's ambassador to France. Homesick, Neruda mails Mario a letter (which he jokes Mario

---

Massimo Troissi, who died shortly after filming was completed. It offers a lush and faithful version of the novel—with the somewhat odd exception of transferring its location from Chile to Italy. For the sake of clarity, my quotations come from Katherine Silver's 1995 English translation of the novel.

will have to deliver to himself) and a tape recorder. Neruda tells Mario:

> It is a present for you. But I also want to ask of you a favor that only you, Mario, can do . . . I want you to take this tape recorder around Isla Negra with you and tape all the sounds and noises you can find. I desperately need something, even if it is only a shadow, from my home. (75)

Neruda goes on to list the kinds of sounds Mario might record—the bells in his garden, the waves crashing on the rocks, the gulls. "And if you hear the silence of the stars, tape it" (76). Mario sets himself to this task with gusto, spending weeks recording tides, birds, bees, barks, and bells before sending Neruda a sound collage that ends, unexpectedly, with the cries of his and Beatriz's newborn son (85–86). It is a poem made not of metaphors but things, of sounds and events.

But that's not all. For Mario also uses this assignment as a kind of pre-writing exercise, composing a brief and lovely poem, "Ode to the Snow over Neruda in Paris," which he sends along with the audiotape (84). The point is not that Mario thus becomes the poetic equal of Neruda. Far from it. But he is someone who, through a kind of sound-writing, can do a favor for Neruda, much as the poet once did a favor for him. Their correspondence is founded on a mutual respect. And that inspires Mario to write, perhaps for the first time, in his own voice.

The novel ends on a bitter note. Mario writes at least one more poem, a sketch of his son, which he submits to a contest run by a left-wing literary journal. But events intervene. Allende's government is overthrown. The presses are shut down. Neruda is called back to Isla Negra and dies a few days after. The next morning two unidentified men take Mario away for questioning. He is disappeared. His poem is lost. The point seems to be that while poetry may fire the hearts of ordinary men and women, it has little effect on those of generals and politicians.

Still, I am struck by what Neruda and Mario achieve together. For if Mario is postman to the poet, Neruda hopes to be the poet of workers, of postmen. The two need each other. They find a way to communicate, to teach and learn, through a kind of gift economy. Neruda offers Mario his metaphors; Mario repays the favor with the sounds of Isla Negra and his own poem. What an extraordinary way to think about teaching, not as work for hire but as a series of favors and requests, of time and attention freely given!

Unfortunately, the relationship between writer and reader, student and teacher, is often far more complex and fraught—even and perhaps especially when the two admire each other. In chapter 4, I turn to several stories of writerly deception and plagiarism.

4

FORGING A SELF

In a scene midway through Curtis Sittenfeld's *Prep* (2005), high school sophomore Lee Fiora gets ready to leave her English class:

> We all stood and gathered our backpacks and I looked around my chair to make sure I hadn't dropped anything. I was terrified of unwittingly leaving behind a scrap of paper on which were written all my private desires and humiliations. (123)

Sittenfeld's novel is a painfully accurate rendering of the self-consciousness of adolescence. Lee is a scholarship student at a tony New England prep school. She has become attuned to the fine distinctions of social rank and anxious to hide the signs of her own middle-class background. Writing is for her a chance to slip up, to reveal traces of a self she is working to leave behind.

But, of course, writing also offers you the chance to forge a new self, one you can manage and fashion in ways everyday life rarely allows. You can become a different person on the page or at least sound like one. That is, I suspect, one reason behind the interest so many novels and films take in the teaching of writing. The stakes seem higher than in most other subjects, in math or science or social studies. For what is being learned is not simply a skill but a form of self-expression and perhaps of self-making.

Which, in turn, raises the possibility of deception. What ties the person we hear on the page to the actual person writing? How do we tell if the voice created on a page by a writer is authentic or fraudulent? The smith forges something new out of iron and fire; the grifter forges a check, a signature, an identity.

Later in this chapter I'll look at several novels about students who want so badly to become writers they are willing to

DOI: 10.7330/9781607329725.c004

compromise who they are as persons. In Francine Prose's *Blue Angel* (2000), a talented and opportunistic young woman is so eager to publish her work that she concocts an elaborate scheme to entrap her writing teacher. In May Sarton's *The Small Room* (1961), a young scholar so desperately wants to impress her mentor that she plagiarizes her thesis. And in Tobias Wolff's *Old School* (2004), a likable and ambitious young man so identifies with a short story written by another student that he convinces himself that it is his own. Each of these novels portrays a plagiarist who aims not so much to deceive as to become someone they are not quite yet. But first let me return to the other side of the problem, as it were, to *Prep* and Lee Fiora's worries that her writing will instead disclose the very person she no longer wants to be.

CIPHERS

Lee Fiora is not an especially sympathetic person. She is an arriviste, a born social climber, who as a fourteen-year-old conceives the ambition to attend boarding school as a way to escape the boredom of her home in South Bend, Indiana. *Prep* chronicles the four years she spends at the fictional Ault School in Massachusetts. During that time, Lee distances herself from anyone who might impede her efforts to become a preppy insider—an Asian roommate, an African American classmate, a working-class townie who asks her for a date, her mother and father when they visit for Parents' Weekend. But Lee is not so much conniving as desperate not to be found out. She yearns to blend in, which makes her an extremely sharp observer of what goes on at Ault.

Lee's teacher for sophomore English is another outsider—Ms. Moray, twenty-two years old, a recent graduate of the University of Iowa, smart but naive, an earnest midwesterner thrown among the eastern sophisticates of Ault. Lee, of course, loathes her immediately. She hates her sincerity, her enthusiasm, her careful attempts to dress like a prep school teacher. For Lee, these shortcomings are symbolized by a silver pin shaped like a book with its pages turned open that Ms. Moray often wears to class. It seems a "frumpy accessory" to Lee, something probably given to her by an older relative or teacher and now a clear sign that Ms. Moray is just trying a little too hard to fit in (117).

Near the start of the semester, after the class has read *Walden*, Ms. Moray assigns students to write an essay on where they go to reflect on life. But after listening to her classmates read descriptions of their houses in Scarsdale and their boats on the Long Island Sound, Lee has a mild panic attack. She cannot force herself to read her essay aloud in class. Ms. Moray excuses her for the moment but then insists that Lee read her piece to her alone after class. Her essay begins with a few throat-clearing sentences about Thoreau and solitude. It then moves to the passage Lee realized she could not read to her classmates:

> My father's store is called Mattress Headquarters. It is located in South Bend, Indiana . . . In the back of the store, there is an office and behind the office, there is a storage room with many mattresses. This [is] the room where I reflect because it is quiet and comfortable, and I could lie on all the mattresses, which sometimes reached almost to the ceiling. The best part of this room is that I can hear other people talking, especially my father because he has a loud voice. I can listen to my father and other people such as customers and sales staff and know I am not alone, yet I do not have to join in the conversation. (136)

Lee has let her guard down. Her father is in trade. She has handed in the very scrap of paper she fears others might discover, the one that lists her secrets and humiliations. But Ms. Moray either fails to recognize the source of Lee's anxiety or refuses to acknowledge it. Instead, she praises the essay, "especially . . . the part about being able to hear your father's voice" (136), and tells Lee that it's good to meet a fellow midwesterner. She decides that what Lee really needs is "Confidence," which she mouths encouragingly to Lee, thrusting her arms out like a cheerleader (137).

Ms. Moray is right, of course, but Lee is well beyond the reach of pep talks from her teachers. She has no intention of becoming a model student. Rather, she wants to remake herself in the image of her privileged classmates, which means writing not more but less about her actual life and views. The next assignment in sophomore English is to "write about something that mattered to us, to take a stand" (138), and Lee is stumped. There's not really all that much she cares about, besides fitting in at school. She comes up with a phony piece on why "Prayer Is Not a Good Idea in Public Schools." Irritated, Ms. Moray fails Lee's essay, although it is probably no worse than the pieces on abortion or travel or sports written by her classmates. But Ms. Moray had hoped for more from Lee, for some sign of commitment or interest. As she tells her after class: "I don't know what to do with you, Lee. I don't understand you. You're a cipher" (161).

Here Ms. Moray perhaps says more than she intends, for the term *cipher* defines Lee in several senses. She is a riddle, a code her teacher can't crack. She has sealed herself off from the gaze or friendship of others. And she also feels like a person of no consequence, a nobody. What matters to Lee is the gap she senses between herself and her more assured classmates: "All I ever did was watch other students and feel curious about them and feel dazzled by their breeziness and wracked by the impossible gaping space between us, my horrible lack of ease, my inability to be casual" (162). But that gap is not something she can write about.

Or at least not at that moment in her life. *Prep* is told from the perspective of Lee ten years or so after she graduates from Ault—and this older Lee is able to find words for emotions and insights that her younger self cannot yet articulate. A weakness of *Prep* as a novel is that it never shows *how* Lee develops this ability. Her encounter with Ms. Moray ends in an uneasy truce, but Lee never shows any stirrings of intellectual interest in her class or in any of the others she takes at Ault.

The older Lee does possess an empathy her younger self lacks. Remembering the silver pin, the badge of reading, that Ms. Moray used to wear, she now sees that

> she was a young woman who had moved alone to a different part of the country, and she must have been acutely conscious of all these factors—that she was young, that she was a woman, that

she was alone; her happiness, if she was happy (I have no idea
if Ms. Moray was happy), must have felt so tenuous. That is why,
looking back, I am almost sure she bought the pin for herself.
(165–66)

It's a poignant observation. If the young Lee is a cipher,
Ms. Moray is an open book. She identifies with writing, while
Lee believes "written words trapped you" (147). Ms. Moray's
mistake lies in thinking she can will Lee into becoming someone like her. She is a failed dead poet who has picked the wrong
student to try to inspire.

It's tempting to speculate that Lee is someone who might be
drawn to more critical or analytic sorts of writing—that what she
fears is not writing so much as the disclosure of emotion, of self.
But I'm not sure there's a clear lesson in teaching to be drawn
from *Prep*—except perhaps for a caution against remaking students in our own images. And yet that is precisely what so many
teachers in novels and films seem to do.

DECEIVERS

Angela Argo is an unlikely siren. Skinny, awkward, clad in motor-
cycle leather and chains, her red hair streaked with orange and
green, her "sharp-featured face pierced in a half-dozen places"
(8), the emo-punk Angela has sat silently for weeks in Ted
Swenson's fiction writing class. Swenson is yet another middle-
aged writer who has stopped writing; it's been years since he
published his second novel, and he has long lost interest in
working on his third. But he's also a serious teacher and a likable guy, happy in his marriage and his teaching job at a small
New England college. Angela finally speaks up and saves a class
discussion Swenson has let go off the rails. She's a more perceptive and candid reader than her classmates. She's also at work
on a novel, which she asks Swenson to read. It's good, and he
takes an interest in her. And so Francine Prose would seem to
prime us for a classic wonder boy narrative in *Blue Angel* (2000).

But the title of her novel suggests otherwise—since it invokes
The Blue Angel (1930), a classic early sound film directed by Josef

von Sternberg, in which a staid professor wrecks his career in mad pursuit of a cabaret singer, Lola, played by none other than Marlene Dietrich.[1] So this Angela must clearly be trouble. And indeed, as Swenson falls head over heels for her, we realize that she is manipulating what goes on, creating a situation where he will feel compelled to take her writing to his publisher.

But even though their relationship quickly involves sex, or at least a failed attempt at it, Swenson is more driven by an intellectual lust. He seems indifferent to Angela's thin body and edgy appearance; at one point, he describes her as a "twitchy ferret" (49). It is her skill as a writer that attracts him. Prose provides several excerpts of Angela's novel in progress, "Eggs," which is, aptly enough, about an affair between a student and a teacher. It's funny and erotic in a slightly creepy manner, and despite his own warnings to students not to read fiction as disguised autobiography, Swenson can't help but speculate about possible real-life sources of the story. He lets Angela flatter him—she admires his writing, his is the only course she bothers to attend—and he listens to her stories about her boyfriend and her parents. He discovers she has written a series of poems about a phone sex worker and secretly reads them. He is so seduced by everything Angela says and writes that it never occurs to him that all of it, not just her novel, may be made up. She has forged a self, a persona, that she lives out not just on the page but in her daily life.

Blue Angel ends with Swenson hauled before a campus judicial board to face charges of sexual harassment brought by Angela. Such board hearings are staples of fiction about teaching. Four of the texts I discuss in this book (*Educating Rita, Oleanna, Mustang Sally, Blue Angel*) include scenes in which teachers are grilled by committees about their behavior, as do several other recent academic novels—including J. M. Coetzee's *Disgrace* (1999) and Philip Roth's *The Human Stain* (2000). But I think the scene misfires in *Blue Angel*. One of Prose's aims seems to be to satirize the political correctness of the academy in the

---

1. In 2017 *Blue Angel* was itself made into a film, *Submission*, directed by Richard Levine—in some sense completing the circle from film to book to film again. It is a faithful but unfortunately lackluster adaptation.

1990s, and I suspect that Swenson's trial is supposed to achieve a kind of madcap absurdity, as a procession of friends, colleagues, and students betray him with increasingly wild accusations—but it all just seems kind of sad. Prose's characters are too human and personable to function as satiric figures.

That includes Angela Argo. However conniving she may be, Angela is also an inventive writer, confident in her sexuality, and witty in the design of her ploys to deceive Swenson. She's a compelling, well-realized character. You can understand why Swenson falls for her. He sees in her another version of himself—not in the sense that she might also achieve what he has already done but that she represents what he hopes to become again. Swenson sees in her a way of renewing his life as a writer. There's a quiet and wonderful scene in *Blue Angel* in which, having read several chapters of Angela's novel, Swenson returns to his own work in progress. It now bores him. He's more interested in what Angela is writing.

And in what Angela has to say. In the beginning pages of the novel, Swenson defines his problem in leading a writing workshop:

> Let his colleagues try this. The ones who think it's easy—no lengthy texts, no lectures, no exams to grade. . . . Let them spend class knowing their careers depend on finding a way to chat about bestiality so that no one's feelings get hurt. (4–5)

For sex with animals has been a recurring theme in the stories written for Swenson's course that semester. His students aren't sexual outlaws; they're just looking for ways to impress their teacher, push the envelope—while he's searching for a way to have a civil conversation with them about writing technique. In this particular class, the students patter on about plausible ways of explaining why the narrator of a short story they are discussing, rebuffed by his girlfriend, might relieve his sexual tensions at the end of the evening with the aid of a refrigerated chicken. Swenson knows that for such a story to have any chance of working, the narrator's actions must not only come as a surprise but also feel like the sort of thing any of us might, at some point, be capable of doing. But he's not sure how to say as much to a group of near-adolescents. And so when Angela awakes from her silence and remarks

> I guess I think the best thing—the one good thing—is that the end is so weird and unexpected. Isn't that the point? Anyone could do something like this. (10)

Swenson is thrilled. Angela can say to her peers what he cannot. She becomes his second and more eloquent voice.

Prose illustrates the tensions of a writing workshop in accurate and comic ways. She sketches quick portraits of Swenson's students without caricaturing them and shows how they compete with one another for his praise while guarding against criticisms that seem too frank or hostile. "Attentive to infinitesimal shifts of status and position" (113), they note how Swenson defers to Angela in class and resent that she doesn't share any of her own work in progress. When Angela finally does bring in a chapter from her novel, they suspend their customary rule of politeness and trash it. Swenson foolishly rushes in to defend her work against their criticisms, arguing that they have failed to appreciate its originality, which, of course, only causes "two dark coals of resentment [to] glow in each student's face" (203).

Swenson's self-deception enables Angela's scheme. He is happy to have her become a stand-in for his views in class. Although warned she is unstable and prone to making up stories, he believes everything she tells him. He identifies so strongly with her work that he fails to notice that she, too, is writing sort of a sex with animals story. (The student in her novel is incubating eggs for a science project; at a key moment there is need for lubrication . . .) And all of this is because Swenson is convinced Angela "may be a real writer" (134)—which, in turn, would seem to make him a real teacher. Angela doesn't need to sleep with Swenson to convince him to show her novel to his publisher. Doing so merely seals the deal and then turns everyone against him when things begin to sour.

As teachers, we live on through the work of our students. Novels like *Prep* and *Blue Angel* speak to the importance of keeping that statement in the plural. There is hubris involved in imagining you can divine who among a group of young and unformed writers possesses true talent. Swenson's intellectual infatuation with Angela warps the way he teaches his seminar. He becomes invested in proving, if only to himself, that she is a better writer than anyone else in the room. Angela takes advantage of his credulity. The deception at the heart of *Blue Angel* is the result of a *folie à deux*, the willingness of both to believe that Angela possesses a genius that separates her from her classmates.

PLAGIARISM

Like *Dead Poets Society*, May Sarton's 1961 novel, *The Small Room*, is preoccupied with what it means to be a good teacher. Also like *Dead Poets*, *The Small Room* is set in a single-sex school in New England, although in this case it is a women's college rather than a boys' prep school. At that point the similarities fade. The atmosphere of Appleton College in *The Small Room* is scholarly, intense, cloistered; there are no teachers jumping up on desks. On the contrary, in a powerful chapter, we see a class begin not with a "dramatic opening" but its "exact opposite" (112), as a senior professor turns from the window to ask her students:

> You have all read some of the Keats letters. Would one of you like to read a passage aloud, or a whole letter that you think appropriate for class discussion? (112)

The rest of the chapter shows the professor artfully leading her students through the letters, working with the passages they have chosen, highlighting and connecting themes as they arise, before finally closing the class by reading a few excerpts from Keats that she has herself selected. Her students move with her not toward a self-understanding, an epiphany of the *Dead Poets* sort, but toward a deeper understanding of a subject outside of themselves. It is an extraordinary class, one of the few I have read in fiction that I would want to take as a guide for my own work as a teacher.

Lucy Winter, the protagonist of the novel, is a quiet and observant young woman who has just broken off an engagement and, unsure of what she wants to do next, has come to teach for a year at Appleton. A few weeks into her first semester, Lucy stumbles upon a case of plagiarism. The protégé of the most respected professor on campus has copied much of her piece for *Appleton Essays* from an obscure article by Simone Weil that Lucy happens to have read. There is an initial attempt to cover up the incident after Lucy reluctantly reports it, but word soon gets out in the small college community, and both the professor and the student are shamed.

It's clear that the student plagiarizes out of a desire not to deceive but to impress her mentor. What is valued at Appleton is not self-expression but a passionate commitment to scholarship. Still, professors and students alike wonder about the personal costs of such devotion. As the student confides to Lucy about her work with her mentor:

> From the time I first had her as a Sophomore she has been at me to produce, produce, produce . . . The more you do, the more you're expected to do, and each thing has got to be better, always better. (100)

Such pressures don't excuse plagiarism, and the student in this case is clearly troubled and confused. In trying to prove that she really is the sort of scholar her mentor expects, she traduces what both of them hold dear. If she had cared less, she would not have plagiarized. This is the irony Sarton explores with such skill and nuance. We long for the affection and praise of our teachers or our students, but we can only gain it from them indirectly, through the work we do with a subject. For the moment we ask directly for their friendship or their love, we are no longer teacher and student.

Lucy comments on this paradox later on in the novel. The students in her introductory literature class invite her to tea near the end of the semester and, as is so often the case, the event falls flat. Even though Lucy's students like and respect her, they have no idea how to make small talk with her. How could they? As she is getting ready to leave, Lucy tells them:

What you want, I would guess, is to make contact with the human being, with me myself, not Professor Winter. And this is possible sometimes between a student and a professor, but . . . Maybe it can only be done *after* that particular relationship has ended. In the classroom, you see, there are three entities present, you the class, me, and a third far greater than we who fuses us at moments into a whole. When that third is absent, our real relationship falls apart. (216–17)

Lucy is surely correct that the job of a teacher is to connect with students *in relation to a subject*—much as, earlier in the novel, we saw happen in her colleague's class on Keats's letters. There is a bond but also a needed impersonality or reserve. The plagiarism case that drives the plot of *The Small Room* shows, though, how difficult it can be to sustain such a relationship—particularly as a student grows to admire and identify with her teacher and her teacher begins to see herself in her protégé. The connection they feel for each other starts to displace their focus on the subject that first brought them together.

I suspect it may be especially hard to maintain such an emotional reserve when the subject of instruction is writing. Our work as writers is bound up tightly with who we are or want to be. The third entity Lucy speaks of, the subject that lies outside both teacher and students, is not present, I think, in quite the same way in a writing class as it is in a course on literature or anthropology or history. The work on the table is likely to feel more closely tied to both teacher and students—particularly when what they are discussing is a writer's style, the eloquence or persuasiveness of their approach. The situation is complicated even more by the understandable tendency of aspiring writers to want to sound like the established writers they most admire. You want to forge your own voice as a writer; you just also hope that voice sounds something like Ernest Hemingway or Alice Walker or your professor.

CRYPTOMNESIA

Tobias Wolff's *Old School* (2004) centers on this tension between imitation and originality. The unnamed narrator of the novel is a senior at an (also unnamed) boys' prep school in 1960. Like

Lee in *Prep*, he is not one of the patrician East Coast WASPs who set the tone of his school. Rather, he is working class and part Jewish—both of which he does his best to hide. But unlike Lee, he identifies wholeheartedly with the intellectual ethos of his school. He yearns to be a writer, and as he puts it, "if the school had a snobbery it would confess to, this was its pride in being a literary place" (4). Three times a year the school is visited by a distinguished author. Before each of these visits, the students in the senior class are invited to submit a piece of writing to be read by the guest author, who selects from them one boy to meet with privately.

The idea is that you develop your own voice as a writer through apprenticing yourself to a master—learning to write in their cadences and diction, to work with their sort of themes and characters and preoccupations. In the year of the novel, the first author to visit the school is Robert Frost, and so the boys busy themselves trying to write poems both homespun and elegiac. The problem lies in finding something to write *about* that seems to fit with this approach to verse. Unfortunately, it doesn't seem to occur to any of the boys that Frost was writing from his own experience. Instead, they try to invent the details of scenes they know next to nothing about. The narrator, for instance, writes a poem about elk hunting—although he has never been hunting or seen an elk. He is simply trying to evoke a sense of wintry stoicism.

The contest is won by the narrator's friend George Kellogg, an earnest type, the editor of the school literary magazine, who writes a "dramatic monologue in which an old farmer feels the bite of mortality on the first cold day of autumn" (39). The poem begins with the old farmer's thoughts as he ogles a young hired girl milking a cow, watching her soft hands "pull the foaming cream into the pail between her legs," and ends as he strides off, philosophizing, into an early snow (39). George titles it "First Frost."

To the surprise of everyone, though, the actual Frost reads George's poem not as an homage but a gentle burlesque. As the distinguished poet tells a reporter for the school newspaper:

Young Kellogg has had some fun at this old man's expense, and I guess this old man can stand some fun, if it isn't too expensive. He said he liked the joke of the milkmaid having soft hands. *All the milkmaids I've ever had to do with could've gone bare-knuckle with Jim Corbett and made him bleed for his purse.* Frost suggested that a few winters on a farm wouldn't hurt any young poet, *to learn that snow is no metaphor, if nothing else. But I've dipped my bucket there a time or two, and your young fellow Kellogg has caught me fair and square.* (40)

Poor George. Frost is unable to see his poem as a serious imitation of his work and so reads it as parody. Luckily, his good humor covers for his misunderstanding. He pays George the complement of seeming far more sophisticated than he actually is. But Frost is also only able to read the boy's poem as a comment on his own writing—which leads him to misread George as much as George misappropriates him. Frost doesn't see that the real themes of George's poem are the teenage warhorses of horniness and fear of death. The joke is on both of them. Frost turns George into an ironist; George turns Frost into a back porch versifier.

The next visiting author misreads the work of her contest winner all the more comically. This is Ayn Rand, cheerleader for unchecked individualism and author of *The Fountainhead* and *Atlas Shrugged*, who has been invited in an attempt to curry favor with a wealthy alumnus of the school. Rand chooses a story by Big Jeff Purcell, a likable oddball, the only vegetarian in the senior class, and an advocate of interplanetary exploration. Big Jeff has fused his two enthusiasms in a story called "The Day the Cows Came Home," in which he imagines that the Earth has been invaded by a race of super-bovines from outer space who exact a terrifying price for our long-term carnivorous mistreatment of cows. But all Rand sees in this vegetarian fantasy of revenge is a reflection of her own crackpot philosophy, in which, as she puts it, "the herd denies the truth of its own enslaved condition, and attacks the heroic truth-teller" (78). This leads to a hilarious exchange between her and Big Jeff, who rises to his feet during her public appearance at the school to ask:

Miss Rand, your books reach thousands of people—
Millions.

> Millions of people. Just think what a difference it would make if they knew your position on meat. (87)

Rand, of course, has no clue as to what Jeff is talking about. "Meat?" she says. "What depraved psychology prompts you to speak like this to the author of *Atlas Shrugged*?" (87). Angry and confused, she quits the room, her entourage following.

Imitating another writer thus proves more complicated than it might at first seem. George and Big Jeff are able to produce writing that *sounds* something like Frost or Rand, but they don't really understand *what* they're imitating. They have the manner but not the substance. However sincere their efforts, they thus produce something closer to parody than imitation. Ironically, though, it's this unintended gap between the work of the student and the master that lends their writing its charm. For it is in the *differences* between George and Frost, Jeff and Rand—even when they result from a lack of skill or maturity—that we begin to sense the distinctive personalities of the students. Both boys end up writing in their own voices by accident, as it were, through trying to write like somebody else.

But what propels the novel is the announcement that Ernest Hemingway will be the third author to visit the school that year. Wolff's narrator idolizes Hemingway. In fact, to understand what it would feel like to write like Hemingway, he has retyped several of the master's short stories, page by page. So he is determined to win a meeting with his hero.

Unfortunately, that doesn't mean he's able to come up with a story in Hemingway's vein. In fact, as the deadline for submission looms, he's stuck. Alone late one night in the office of the school's literary journal, the narrator leafs through a stack of back issues of journals from other New England prep schools, all filled with similarly predictable stories, until to his surprise he stumbles on one that arrests him, "Summer Dance," a story published five years before in a review from a private girls' school.

What engages the narrator is both the matter-of-fact tone of the story and its subject; it is about a middle-class Jewish girl trying to fit into a WASP culture. The story begins with the sentence, "I hope nobody saw me pick the cigarette butt off the sidewalk . . ." (122), and the narrator is hooked. The story continues, documenting the small indignities of belonging to a lower social class. As the narrator explains:

> The whole thing came straight from the truthful diary I'd never kept: the typing class, the bus, the apartment; all mine. And mine too the calculations and stratagems, the throwing over of old friends for new . . . And, yes, the almost physical attraction to privilege, the resolve to be near it at any cost: sycophancy, lies, self-suppression, the masking of ambitions and desires, the slow cowardly burn of resentment toward those for whose favor you have falsified yourself. Every moment of it was true. (125–26)

The narrator begins retyping. The story astonishes him because it is actually written from the point of view of a prep school student—not an elk hunter or a New England farmer or a witness to an interplanetary invasion. It feels authentic, without pretense, without a mask, like Hemingway except in high school. It is what he wishes he was capable of writing now. He keeps typing, obsessively, through the night and into the dawn, only changing a few necessary details—names, locations, "other particulars" (126):

> I finished the story just before the bell rang before breakfast. I read it through and fixed a few typos, but otherwise it needed no correction. It was done. Anyone who read this story would know who I was. (127)

So who is this person who has been laid bare upon the page? In one sense, it is a fraud, someone who has almost unconsciously retyped and claimed the work of another writer as his own. But in another sense, the story does indeed show us the narrator—a boy who desperately wants to be accepted, to fit in, but who is painfully, nervously aware of the shortcomings of his background and temperament. And in still another sense, the story reveals the narrator as someone so eager to call himself a writer that he is willing to become someone else to do so.

Events unravel. Hemingway picks the narrator's plagiarized story from the others sent to him. It's published in the school paper, with a comment from Papa saying, in part, "He is writing cleanly and well about what he knows and he's writing from his conscience" (135). The narrator's friends are surprised by the unvarnished quality of his story while also envious that he was able to tell it. As one of them tells him, with unknowing irony, "If I hadn't seen your name on it I wouldn't have thought it was yours" (138). But the inevitable occurs. Someone has read the original version of the story. The narrator is summoned to the headmaster's office and quickly expelled from school.

What is hard to convey in summary but is clear in the novel is that the narrator is not a cynic. He really does identify with the story he has plagiarized. It *felt* like his own, or at least it did during the first, frenzied activity of (re)writing it. But when confronted, he immediately sees and admits the story is not his—except in the sense that it spoke directly and powerfully to him. The narrator owns his guilt, accepts his punishment, leaves school, works at odd jobs, and joins the army—all the while still harboring dreams of becoming a writer. A few years later, he rereads the story and is moved to write a note of apology to its actual author, Susan Friedman. To his surprise, she writes back, saying "plagiarism, not imitation, is the sincerest form of flattery" (157).

Susan and the narrator meet for lunch. It's an awkward meeting. She is five years older than him, a second-year medical student, much more sophisticated, and inclined to view the theft of her story as a "prank" rather than a life-altering event. She's amused that "Papa himself couldn't tell if he was reading the story of a boy or a girl" (161) and unimpressed by the literary life, which strikes her as frivolous. When the narrator insists that her story is "brave and honest," she replies, "How do you know it isn't a sham from start to finish" (162).

So once again we stumble upon a gap in interpretation between student and author. The narrator has plagiarized Susan, almost word for word. But his attitude toward her story remains too reverential for her taste. What was for her a "well-written little exercise" (162) was for him a revelation of self (although *whose* self exactly is never clear). The narrator describes Susan as poised and gracious. So it could be that she dismisses her story, at least in part, as a way of offering them a way out of a difficult conversation, of saying that what is past is past. Even still, it also seems clear that—like Frost with George or Rand with Big Jeff—she feels that her acolyte, her plagiarist, never really quite got what she was trying to say.

I find it telling that *Old School* offers no successful examples of imitation. George's homage to Frost, Big Jeff's vegetarian science fiction, even the narrator's wholesale appropriation of "Summer Dance"—they all end up missing their targets. More important, none of the boys learns to write from his own experience. Near the beginning of the novel, there is a wonderful passage in which the narrator reflects on the one criticism he and his classmates are unwilling to make of each other:

> All of us owed someone, Hemingway or cummings or Kerouac—or all of them, and more. We wouldn't have admitted to it but the knowledge was surely there, because imitation was the only charge we never brought against the submissions we mocked so cruelly. There was no profit in it. Once crystallized, consciousness of influence would have doomed the collective and necessary fantasy that our work was purely our own. (14)

Because they've lived so little, the students are almost forced to mimic the voices and stories of those they've read. But they need to gain more than life experience alone. We learn near the end of the novel that the narrator does eventually become a working writer, but only when, "after much floundering, [he] went to college and worked like the drones he once despised, kept reasonable hours, learned to be alone in a room, learned to throw stuff out, learned to keep gnawing the same bone until it cracked" (156). In other words, he becomes a writer only when, after years of trying to imitate genius, he learns to treat writing instead as a job. *Old School* ends up a pæan to neither talent nor imitation but to craft.

CRAFT

I've returned several times in this book to two competing ways of imagining writing. On the one hand, writing is often pictured as an everyday skill that almost anyone ought to be able to teach or learn. On the other hand, it is also seen as a window onto the self. Writing teachers are thus viewed as either low-level professionals, skills instructors, or as something closer to shamans or priests, guardians of a secret, gatekeepers of a higher realm. I think the novels I've looked at in this chapter begin to offer a way beyond this standoff between the mystical and the mundane. For what they suggest is that learning to write involves becoming not a disciple but an apprentice, that it is an entrance into a craft, a guild, rather than an imitation of genius. As Lucy Winter remarks at the tea party in *The Small Room*, the relationship between a teacher and student needs to be grounded in the study of a subject, in something outside of them. Otherwise, they have nothing to work on together.

But what does it mean to say that when the subject is writing? *Old School* warns against reducing the craft of writing to technique. For while the schoolboys in Wolff's novel possess the skill to parrot the phrasings and attitudes of Frost, Rand, or Hemingway, they lack the experience to do work that is meaningfully like the authors they are imitating. In a similar if perhaps more sophisticated way, the young woman caught plagiarizing in *The Small Room* is so driven to impress her mentor that, unsure of what she herself might have to say as a novice scholar, she substitutes the voice of an authority for her own. In both cases, what the student is writing about turns out to matter less than who they are writing for. As for Lee Fiora in *Prep*, there is never really any subject, only a desire to fit in (although in her case with her classmates rather than teachers). Angela Argo in *Blue Angel* is a bit more complicated; she has a true talent but still ends up less interested in what she is writing about than in using her work to seduce and punish her hapless teacher.

What I take away from these novels, then, is that it can be dangerous to focus on craft in the abstract—that what almost always matters is *why* a specific writer uses a certain technique to say something in a particular situation. Or to put this in slightly different terms, to really teach writing as a craft, you need to consider and respond to what an individual writer is trying to accomplish. Otherwise, you are simply repeating formulas.

Jayne Relaford Brown speaks to this need to keep both the writer and her craft constantly in view in her wise and funny poem, "Emily Dickinson Attends a Writing Workshop" (2000). Brown's one-page poem consists of a typewritten version of Dickinson's "My Life had stood—a Loaded Gun," as though it had been submitted as an assignment in a creative writing course, with extensive markings and comments handwritten all over it by an anonymous teacher. These comments are both perfectly ordinary and comically obtuse: "Why all the Caps? (–And dashes?) why a 'loaded' gun?" The teacher also warns against beginning too many lines with "And," reorders Dickinson's stanzas to establish a consistent time line, and cuts the famous closing verse ("For I have but the power to kill / Without—the power to die") as "too confusing." They conclude with a note that begins "Emily—Nice language here but I end this poem feeling confused," before going on to ask, "Is there another poem behind this one that still needs to be written?" In short, the teacher notes all the ways Dickinson violates the conventional techniques of poetry workshops but fails to ask why she does so. Instead, they simply assume that any deviation from the norm is a mistake and then proceed to show Emily how it might be corrected. It is advice that could be given to any writer about any poem.

Of course, the joke here is on the teacher. Dickinson's poem has fascinated so many readers for so long not despite but because of its eccentricities. To revise it according to workshop dictates could only lessen its impact. There is a moment in their closing note when the teacher verges on recognizing as much, writing to Emily that "you seem to be alluding to some anger, yet the cause is never explored or revealed." But that is the very point of the poem. The sense of anger and yearning in Dickinson's poem is haunting precisely because it has no clear origin. She is describing a state of mind or feeling, not telling a story. But to begin to appreciate how she does this, you need first to trust that she knows what she is doing. As the critic I. A. Richards (1942, 41) once advised about approaching a difficult poem, "Read it as though it makes sense and perhaps it will."

But the imagined workshop teacher fails to extend this sort of trust as a reader to Emily. Brown's parody plays upon the lack of respect that lies behind so many teacher comments on student writing. Since we're not convinced that what students have to say is all that new or makes all that much sense, we offer them general tips about writing rather than specific responses to their work. And so Emily—like all those other writers whose ambitions exceed or elude our formulas of response—is left pretty much to her own devices. The workshop has failed her.

Let me be clear. I admire the theories of rhetoric and writing the field of composition has developed. I have tried over the course of my career to contribute to them. But what I take from the books, movies, and plays I have discussed so far in this book—most of them composed not from our point of view as writing teachers but from the vantage of those we teach—is that our theories of discourse gain the most meaning, are set most powerfully into motion, when we connect them to the aims of individual writers. Astronomers may happily predict eclipses without reference to those who happen or not to view them, but writing theorists and teachers need actual writers to make use of their ideas. The allure of teaching writing is that it asks us to connect our ideas about how language works to the attempts of students to write pieces that actually say what they hope to say. Our ideas matter as they are embodied in the writing of our students.

In chapter 5, I look at two fictional accounts of teachers who fail to connect their ideas about writing to the work of students. The first is one of the foundational texts of Western literature and philosophy, Plato's *Phaedrus* (1995), in which Socrates is shown as spinning an elaborate theory of writing and rhetoric at the same time he seems to loose interest in the actual views of the young man he is speaking with. The second is Peter Dimock's fine if overlooked 1990 novel, *A Short Rhetoric for Leaving the Family*, in which we watch a man constructing a modern version of the ancient *Rhetorica ad Herennium* as a way of staving off grief and madness. My sense is that both Plato and Dimock hope to reveal the sterility of rhetoric, of method, when it is not tied to the aims of specific writers. Then, in the brief postscript that follows, I look at yet another reason why teachers seem so depressingly often to substitute a canned response ("Why all the Caps?") for a genuine engagement with student work—which is that they lack the time, support, and training to do any better. Most of the accounts of teaching I've looked at in this book have been intense, direct, one-on-one encounters. In closing, I think it's important to consider why such scenes should stand out from the norm, why they should seem remarkable rather than routine.

5

THE LIMITS OF RHETORIC

In 1997 Marilyn Sternglass published her landmark study of the teaching of writing, *Time to Know Them.* Sternglass had followed the progress of nine adult students at the City College of New York over a span of six years. Only one of these students was white, and all of them could be described as basic or under-prepared writers. Several spoke English as a second language. All of them worked outside jobs while taking classes part-time. And all of them had failed the notorious CUNY WAT (Writing Assessment Test) several times over the years. The WAT was a timed, on-the-spot test of a student's ability to produce a passage of Edited Academic English. Thankfully, it is no longer used, but in the 1990s CUNY students could not take advanced courses without first passing it. The irony was that while all of the students Sternglass worked with struggled to pass the WAT, they were also all successful in completing the writing assignments for the courses they had taken. The test, in other words, was telling most of them that they were unprepared to do the work of courses they had already passed. Through her years of work with these writers, Sternglass assembled a rich trove of data to support a simple and compelling argument: if we offer students enough time and support, they will learn how to write.

But time counted against these students in several ways. As working adults, they needed to divide their time and attention among jobs, family, and school. Most of them also needed time and practice, sometimes years of it, to gain a ready fluency in a language they did not speak at home. They needed, that is, to learn not simply how to put their thoughts into English but how to do so quickly and accurately with the clock ticking on a timed test. And they needed to make timely progress toward their

DOI: 10.7330/9781607329725.c005

degrees or risk losing their academic eligibility and funding. So the time Sternglass argued that students should be allowed was for them a valuable commodity indeed.

But note that *time* in her title applies not to students but to teachers. The students Sternglass studied did their best work in courses that pushed them to connect their writing with their own ideas and experiences. While they may thus need time to learn, *we* need time to know and help them. This profound if quiet insight flies against the common belief that good teachers begin by already knowing who their students are and what they need to learn. It suggests that our work begins instead in listening and response.

In this chapter I look at two failures of listening. I link these failures to what I see as an overconfidence in rhetoric—the belief that what someone really needs in order to write well is a system to follow in doing so. The first text I'll look at is one of the most studied in Western literature and philosophy: Plato's *Phaedrus*, written somewhere around 370 BCE. The second is Peter Dimock's brief and absorbing 1990 novel, *A Short Rhetoric for Leaving the Family*. In both texts a teacher elaborates a detailed rhetoric—that is, a system for speaking effectively and gaining the assent of your listeners. But in neither case does it become clear that the teacher has fully persuaded his own listeners or students. Phaedrus never once gets a chance to give a speech of his own in the dialogue that bears his name, so it's hard to tell what he may have learned or not from Socrates. And Jarlath, the narrator of *A Short Rhetoric*, admits at the end of his long, obsessively detailed discourse that the response he expects from his readers is silence. I am intrigued by these gaps between theory and execution. Both texts, it seems to me, end up pointing to the limits of rhetoric, to those moments when one can no longer depend on a system but must instead listen and respond in the moment.

A (FAILED) LESSON IN WRITING

I can't imagine a much better way to begin talking with a student than:

> Phaedrus, my friend! Where have you been? And where are you going? (1)

Which is, of course, the first line of the *Phaedrus*. Socrates greets Phaedrus as a person in motion, an agent, someone who has both a history (where have you been?) and plans of his own (where are you going?). Perhaps most important, he hails him as his equal, his friend.

Unfortunately, the conversation between the two doesn't continue long in this vein. In the scenes that follow, Socrates and Phaedrus discuss several speeches on the nature of love and try to derive from them some principles of speechwriting or rhetoric. Plato's dialogue is thus, among many things, an account of a lesson in writing—the first I know of in literature. In it Socrates has many moments of wit and eloquence, and Phaedrus shows some appealing flashes of irreverence. But as the impromptu class progresses, each falls more and more into a familiar role—with Socrates waxing didactic as the teacher and Phaedrus growing quiet and acquiescent as his pupil.

And if this is a lesson in writing, it's not a particularly successful one. Phaedrus shows no more signs of being able to produce a good speech at the end of Plato's dialogue than he does at its beginning. Quite the contrary. The longer his conversation with Socrates goes on, the less and less he has to say. I am intrigued by how two brilliant and well-intentioned men talking together can seem to teach each other so little. I'm interested, that is, in reading the *Phaedrus* as a failed writing class.

I realize that to do so, I need to bracket out the very sorts of things most readers have felt Plato's dialogue is all about: the nature of love, the relationship between rhetoric and philosophy, the limits of writing as a medium of expression. But it's the oddly familiar shape and rhythm of the dialogue that most draws my attention. For it seems to me that, as Plato dramatizes it, the conversation between Socrates and Phaedrus goes off track in much the same way many classes in writing continue to go awry today. There is an eerie familiarity to this ancient writing lesson. I think we can learn some things about teaching through tracing not only what gets said in Plato's dialogue but what *happens* in it.

So, then, to quickly recap the "action" of the dialogue: When Socrates runs across him just outside the walls of Athens, Phaedrus is carrying a copy of a speech written by one of Socrates's political and intellectual rivals, Lysias, a logographer, or professional speechwriter. Phaedrus admires the speech and hopes to memorize it. The two men sit down by a stream together, and Socrates presses Phaedrus to read the speech (he doesn't trust Phaedrus's memory). Once Phaedrus has finished reading, Socrates offers several criticisms of the text, arguing that Lysias has actually not said very much about his subject, which has to do with the obsessive aspects of erotic love. A little put out but also a little amused, Phaedrus dares Socrates to do better. Socrates improvises a second speech, which Phaedrus also likes. But Socrates isn't happy with that speech, and so he makes yet another, much longer one, the so-called Great Speech, which finally satisfies him (and Phaedrus yet again) and from which he then derives several general rules of rhetoric before launching into an extended closing digression on speech, writing, and memory. Noting that the heat of the afternoon has died down a bit, the two men share a closing prayer and part ways.

But the charm of the dialogue lies in the moment-by-moment interactions of Socrates and Phaedrus. When they first meet, both men seem in a playful and flirtatious mood. Socrates allows Phaedrus to lead him outside his usual haunts in the city to an idyllic spot under a "chaste-tree" by a stream in the woods (6). As Phaedrus remarks, coyly: "The stream is lovely, pure and clear: just right for girls to be playing nearby" (4). The speech he and Socrates are so interested in is written from the perspective of a man who wishes to seduce a beautiful youth without claiming to be in love with him. When Phaedrus offers to summarize the speech from memory, Socrates tells him instead to "show me what you are holding in your left hand under your cloak, my friend" (3). (Is that a scroll in your pocket, or . . . ?) Love, or something like it, is in the air. Phaedrus produces the scroll and reads Lysias's speech, which is aimed at winning the favors of a younger man, to an older man, Socrates, who is openly flirting with him.

Lyisas's speech begins with a simple proposition: "You understand my situation. I've told you how good it would be for us, in my opinion, if this worked out" (7). The speaker then lists in a business-like manner the many benefits the youth he is propositioning might expect to gain from their affair. When Phaedrus finishes, Socrates exclaims:

> I'm in ecstasy . . . I was looking at you while you were reading and it seemed to me the speech had made you radiant with delight . . . I followed your lead, and following you I shared your Bacchic frenzy. (12)

But Phaedrus will have none of that. He tells Socrates to stop joking around, to say what he really thinks. And what Socrates clearly thinks is that he can make a better speech than this one by Lysias, whom he accuses of just "showing off" by finding various ways to say the same thing in different words (13). So Phaedrus dares Socrates to "stop playing hard to get" and deliver a better speech (15). Teasingly, he asks the older man, "Do you understand the situation?" and threatens never to recite another speech for Socrates again if he doesn't produce one of his own on the spot (15). So Socrates gives in and improvises a speech criticizing the desire of men to possess the youths they lust for, like "wolves love lambs" (22). Midway through, he is so enraptured by the flow of his own words that he stops and asks Phaedrus if he isn't "in the grip of something divine" (18)— even though, a few minutes later, Socrates will, like the lovers he criticizes, begin to regret the rush of emotion that overwhelmed him and decide that he needs to offer another speech in praise of real and chaste love instead.

What I find so appealing, at least at this point in the dialogue, is how readily the two friends banter with each other. Early on, when Phaedrus pretends to worry that he is too amateurish a speaker to do justice to Lyisas's speech, Socrates exclaims, "Oh Phaedrus, if I don't know my Phaedrus I must be forgetting who I am myself" (2). The Phaedrus *he* knows, he goes on to tease, was always "going to recite it even if he had to force an unwilling audience to listen" (3). But Phaedrus has a knack for ironic quotation, and so when Socrates later claims to be no match for

Lysias as a speechmaker, it's his turn to say, "Socrates, if I don't know my Socrates, I must be forgetting who I am myself" (15). The two men speak as intimates, equals. Neither defers to the other; neither silences the other. Instead, their conversation is characterized by a friendly give and take.

But this changes—at precisely the moment, it seems to me, when Socrates comes to believe he knows something about love and rhetoric that Phaedrus does not. He decides he must deliver a second, more perfect speech. This "Great Speech" is a dense monologue that runs for twenty-two pages—or about the same length of the entire conversation preceding it. (In contrast, Lysias's speech is only about five pages long, Socrates's first speech, six.) But it's worth noting a peculiar stutter in Plato's text right before Socrates launches into the Great Speech. Stating that his inner *daimonion* has warned him against the impiety of his first speech, Socrates now disowns it, asserting instead, bizarrely, that its true author is Phaedrus, who "charmed me through your potion into delivering it myself" (25). Even more surprising, Phaedrus fails to dispute this odd charge. Instead, he surrenders his early willingness to banter with his friend for the role of a student eager to listen and learn from his master ("No words could be sweeter to my ears, Socrates . . . Most probably, Socrates" [26])—a meek pose he does not break out of until near the end of the dialogue.

By the time Socrates begins his Great Speech, then, Phaedrus has been linked to two discredited speeches—one by Lysias and the other by Socrates himself—even though Phaedrus has actually written neither. The language of the student is defined by what it fails to accomplish. But what makes things even worse in this case is that it's not Phaedrus who gets to learn from these mistakes. Rather, it is Socrates who delivers the Great Speech as Phaedrus gazes at him, rapt and admiring, like one of the schoolboys in *Dead Poets Society*.

I won't contest the eloquence of the Great Speech, although I am not among its admirers. The thrust of the speech is that even if love is a form of madness, it is a divine one that can lead to wisdom. Socrates begins by stating that he aims to "convince the wise if not the clever" (29) but ends up spending most of his time elaborating a fanciful metaphor of the soul as a chariot pulled by two winged horses—one of which "is good, the other not" (44). The driver must somehow manage this mismatched pair. However random and "clever" that conceit may seem, I find the stance Socrates takes toward the "beautiful boy" addressed in the speech even less convincing. His aim seems less to seduce than to uplift. Unlike Lysias, he shows no interest in what the boy might desire from a romantic relationship with him but aims instead to convince him to want something else, something higher. His attitude is didactic, patronizing.

As is his stance now toward Phaedrus. Immediately after his speech, Socrates gently chides Phaedrus for failing to understand several things, both small and large: the pride of Lysias, the meaning of an obscure idiom, the motives of politicians, and, most important, "what distinguishes good from bad writing" (49–51). Indeed, from this point on in their conversation, very little that Phaedrus has to say merits a reply from Socrates, who goes on to offer two improvised lectures—the first on the rules for good writing, the second on the differences between speech and writing—punctuated by brief affirmations and encouragements from Phaedrus. Consider, for example, this string of responses that Phaedrus makes at this point in the dialogue to a series of claims by Socrates:

> Yes.
> I think I understand.
> Certainly.
> We certainly do.
> Right.
> Clearly.
> What a splendid thing, Socrates, he will have understood if he grasps that!
> Of course. (60)

And so, if the dialogue begins with Socrates asking Phaedrus where he is headed, it ends up following a route that has been set by Socrates alone. Phaedrus drops out of the discussion as someone with something of his own to say. The lessons on writing at the end of the dialogue are presented *to* him, but he is not asked to do anything *with* them. They are lessons about writing but not in writing.

While it is somewhat beside the point, I'd also note that the actual advice Socrates offers about speechwriting is curiously uninspired. I say *curiously* because it so oddly and accurately anticipates the bromides offered by modern handbooks on composition. A good speech, Socrates suggests, should be "put together like a living creature," with a head, body, and legs that are "fitting both to one another and to the whole work" (62). It should thus begin with a preamble that states the issue to be discussed and end with a recapitulation that summarizes what it has been about. In between, the speaker should lay out evidence and arguments for his position (62–67). It's all a template for a kind of early five-paragraph theme (a structure Plato himself seems oddly to ignore in his own writing), and Socrates seems a little bored by his own advice, rushing through a quick series of names and references to get to the point he really wants to make—which is about the differences between writing and speech.

Socrates encapsulates this distinction in the famous tale of Thamus and Theuth—which he seems to invent on the spot. Theuth was the Egyptian god of writing. In Socrates's story, he tells the king of Egypt, Thamus, that writing is "a potion for memory and wisdom" (79). But Thamus rejects this view (he is not as pliant a student as Phaedrus), arguing that writing will instead

> introduce forgetfulness into the soul of those who learn it: they will not practice using their memory because they will put their trust in writing, which is external, and depends on signs that belong to others, instead of trying to remember from the inside, completely on their own. You have not discovered a potion for remembering, but for reminding; you provide your students with the appearance of wisdom, not with its reality. (79–80)

Critics since Derrida (1983) have seized upon the paradox of a critique of writing that comes to us *in* writing. We would not know the importance of "remembering," that is, unless Plato's (written) dialogue first "reminded" us of it. But I am more interested here in the role the story plays in the unfolding conversation between Socrates and Phaedrus. For in responding to the tale of Thamus and Theuth, Phaedrus shows a bit of spunk for a change, kidding Socrates that he's "very good at making up stories from Egypt or wherever you want" (80). But when Socrates then chides him for paying more attention to the origin of the story than to its meaning, Phaedrus immediately backs down, saying, "I deserved that, Socrates. And I agree that the Theban king was correct about writing" (80). He is clearly a student who knows just how far to push the teacher, to assert a note of independence without crossing the line into open disagreement.

And yet, I'm not convinced that his agreement with Socrates is fully sincere. A few pages after telling the story, Socrates decides it's time to wrap up his lesson about writing. As any teacher might, he turns to his student for a summary:

> SO: And now that we have agreed about this, Phaedrus, we are finally able to decide the issue.
>
> PH: What issue is that?
>
> SO: The issue which brought us to this point in the first place. We wanted to examine the attack made on Lysias on account of his writing speeches, and to ask which speeches are written artfully and which not. Now, I think we have answered that question clearly enough.
>
> PH: So it seemed; but remind me again how we did it. (83)

Remind? After having just listened to a story whose entire point hinges on the importance of remembering ideas on your own rather than relying on writing to be reminded of them, Phaedrus, the ever attentive and clever student, now needs to be *reminded* of what's been said? I have to imagine him smiling as he replies to Socrates. It's as if he's asking the teacher if this will be on the quiz. Socrates refuses to go for the bait, answering Phaedrus's request with his own straightforward rehashing of his argument, if perhaps ending on the slightest note of exasperation: "This is the whole point of the argument we have been making" (83).

Of course, the problem is that *we* have not made an argument at all. Socrates has made an argument, to which Phaedrus, with a note of irony here and there, has acquiesced. I find it touching that in his final words of the dialogue, Phaedrus reasserts his status as Socrates's equal: "Make it a prayer for me as well. Friends have everything in common" (86). But the dialogue never really gives him a chance to speak as an equal with Socrates. He reads the speech by Lysias, takes the blame for Socrates's first speech, and spends the final part of the dialogue mostly searching for different ways to say "how true" or "I agree."

And so, I read the *Phaedrus* as a cautionary tale. Socrates, it seems to me, suffers from what the literary critic Stanley Fish (1990) has called "theory hope." He thinks he can help Phaedrus learn how to make a better speech by formulating a set of rules, a rhetoric, for doing so. He replaces Lysias as a model with himself and, despite his early flirtatiousness with Phaedrus, does not seem seriously interested in listening to much that the younger man has to say. There is a revealing moment midway through the dialogue, for instance, when Socrates pauses long enough to ask Phaedrus, "And if you have anything else to add about the art of speaking?" But when Phaedrus replies, "Only minor points, not worth making," this allows Socrates to say "well, let's leave minor points aside" (68) and turn back to his own argument. Phaedrus is left without even minor points of his own to make.

It might be argued that Plato's dialogue itself works differently—that in allowing us to notice how Socrates steamrolls over Phaedrus, he opens up the possibility of imagining a different sort of conversation. I'd like to think that, but I still believe we first need to admit that the dialogue shows just how long it has been that teachers have preferred listening to themselves rather than to their students. There is a difference between having a conversation and simply having an audience for your ideas. People interested in student-centered teaching often praise a style of give-and-take inquiry they idealize as the Socratic Method. But the *Phaedrus* dramatizes nothing like an open-ended conversation. My worry is that, in fact, we still do approach the teaching of writing too much in the manner of Socrates. Yes, we need to ask students where they've been and where they're going. We also need to learn to pause for an answer.

PLEASURED SPEECH

The good man, skilled in speaking. Attributed by Quintilian to Marcus Cato the Elder, this was the aim of instruction in classical rhetoric. The phrase also serves as an epigraph for Peter Dimock's brief, difficult, and moving novel, *A Short Rhetoric for Leaving the Family.* Like the *Phaedrus*, *A Short Rhetoric* takes the form of a lesson in writing. The novel is set in 1990, during the buildup to the first Gulf War. Jarlath Lanham writes a letter to his nephew, General, and to his ward, Des, bequeathing his share of the family estate to them once they attain their majority (in 2001). The estate is substantial, and it is hinted that Des may actually be Jarlath's son. Jarlath is prohibited by a legal agreement from seeing both boys. The only thing he asks in return for his behest is that they read the instructions in rhetoric that form the body of his long and meandering letter.

Jarlath is half-mad with grief and guilt. He is the son of one of the principal planners of the Vietnam War, whom he calls simply Father and who closely resembles McGeorge Bundy, the prominent New England WASP who advised Presidents Kennedy and Johnson during the escalation of the war. Like Bundy, Father was the author of two secret memos directly responsible for involving the United States more fully in the war—the first advocating a "Policy of Sustained Reprisal" against the Vietnamese populace, the second arguing for the increased use of combat troops and air strikes. (Jarlath quotes verbatim from Bundy's real-life memos, which were first made public in the *Pentagon Papers.*) The reason for both types of escalation was political expediency: Bundy/Father knew the war was un-winnable but felt it would doom LBJ's presidency to admit as much. Jarlath considers Father a war criminal. In addition, his brother, AG, was an army officer in Vietnam who seems to have allowed his men to collect human ears as souvenirs of combat.

Jarlath has been institutionalized a number of times, unable to cope with his inability to confront his father about the atrocities he put into motion. He writes his *Short Rhetoric* as an attempt to help Des and General do what he could not: speak truth to power. As he urges them, "Practice some method of direct address with which to produce sound in the pleasured mouth for another history" (34).

But once again he fails. For while Jarlath is obsessed with articulating what he calls, in the first line of his letter, "a reliable method of direct address" (5), he is unable to follow one in his own writing. His "reliable method" turns out to be a version of the *Rhetorica ad Herennium*, the oldest surviving Latin treatise on rhetoric, from about 80 BCE. While sometimes attributed to Cicero, the distinguished Roman statesman and author, the *ad Herrenium* is usually considered too pedestrian to be his work. It is most noted for its discussion of memory, which suggests that orators create a series of visual backgrounds and images that will help them remember and order what they want to say (a technique now commonly known as creating a Memory Palace). Jarlath seizes on this system, using five photographs from the Vietnam War as backgrounds and five family scenes as images. One of these photos is the famous image of a Buddhist monk setting himself on fire; another is of Hanoi under American assault; still another is of AG with his soldiers, one of whom holds a necklace made of severed ears.

But the method gets the better of him. While Jarlath describes each photo and scene over and over, he is never able to use them to create a "direct address" to Father, to speak capably against what he knows has been done. Instead, his memories interrupt and overwhelm his attempts at speech.

Indeed, several of the scenes Jarlath employs for his memory system describe moments of speechlessness. Jarlath tells of watching Father's lover attempt suicide (by immolating herself, like the monk in the photo) without being able to shout or run to help her (36–37). (Father rescues her.) He recalls storming into Father's office, eager at last to confront him—"I wanted Father to have to say something about AG, and I would answer"

(60)—but instead being reduced to a wordless rage, reaching across the desk and "grabbing and briefly holding the white softness of the front of Father's shirt" (27). (Security intervenes.) The last time he is permitted to see Des and General, he places the five photos he has been guarding so carefully in a mesh bag attached to a kite they are flying together. When Father and AG rush toward them (they are afraid Jarlath may harm the boys), he releases the kite and the photos into the thin air. The book ends with Jarlath sitting by Father as he lies dying, confused and unable to communicate. Each of these scenes marks a failure of language. Jarlath never leaves the family. He never makes any sort of skilled or "pleasured" speech.

He does argue, though, that all these events occurred before he formulated his method:

> If you take nothing else from this moment of direct address, take this possibility: that the possession of an ornamented style may be all you need. If ever you, too, should find it necessary to leave the family, consider that you may not have to wait for something more in order to speak. (100)

And so, Jarlath continues to place his faith in system, in "the constant application of a practiced mind" (80). He hopes his rhetoric will enable Des and General to speak in ways he could not: "Without an applied art of rhetoric, this task cannot be done" (57).

I find this faith both moving and misguided. Jarlath is a witness to evil and atrocity. He understands that for the sake of political gain, his Father cynically helped to engineer a war he knew was un-winnable and that his brother participated in its horrors. And he is ashamed to admit that "we lived those years without speaking the family history all of us knew" (78). But still, he hopes these failures of human empathy and courage can be atoned for by a theory of "careful speech for another history" (101).

To be fair, Jarlath is aware that "theory without continuous practice in speaking is of little avail" (31). And unlike Socrates, who has Phaedrus right in front of him but shows little interest in what he might have to say, Jarlath seems to hold real affection and respect for Des and General. To some degree, he also seems to realize that he has become captive to the images and scenes he revisits so compulsively, and he urges the boys not to simply use his system but to create images of their own "for your own progress in this art of pleasured speech" (21). But the terms of his release from the hospital do not permit him to meet in person with Des and General, and so, in the end, all he can offer them is his theory, a method, a long and meandering letter in which he obsessively recycles an old Latin treatise on rhetoric. Even he seems to glimpse the futility of this project, as he tells Des and General in the last paragraph of his letter, "If I do not hear from either of you, I will understand" (114).

One of the key terms in Jarlath's thinking is *pleasured*. He repeats the word time and again: "pleasured speech," "a pleasured style," "the pleasured air," "a pleasured man." But it's not a word I've ever seen used in other discussions of rhetoric or writing, and Jarlath never says exactly what he means by it. I suspect, though, that he offers a clue to its definition when, near the end of his letter, he mentions that "I sometimes thought of calling my method Some Speech for Father Descending in Asia: The Pleasure of Rule" (94). For while Jarlath fears and hates Father, he also admires his ability to act, to shape events to his will, or pleasure. Jarlath aims for a similarly *pleasured* shaping of language; he suggests, for instance, that an "ornamented style" may also exhibit a "pleasure of rule" (99). *Pleasured speech* is thus language controlled by the speaker and through which he controls events. It is an ineffectual man's dream of power.

Like Socrates, Jarlath imagines a rhetoric that can solve the problem of writing or speaking in advance. The good man, he believes, if properly trained, will not be stopped speechless before events, will not have to resort to physically attacking his Father across his desk, but will rather be able to call upon the images and scenes he has stored in his memory to make an argument that "will secure, as far as possible, the agreement of your hearers" (101). The poignancy of the novel stems from our realization that no method alone can make that happen.

I am aware of shortchanging *A Short Rhetoric for Leaving the Family* by reading it simply as a lesson in writing. What Jarlath hopes to teach through his rhetoric is not the same thing Peter Dimock hopes to achieve in his novel. Jarlath hopes to construct a system, a rhetoric, that will allow him to cope with the pain his life and family have brought him. Dimock's novel reveals the madness and futility of trying to do so. (Although I suspect that, in some other ways, Dimock's goals are not entirely unlike Jarlath's—that he also hopes his novel will help keep the political cynicism that led to the escalation of the Vietnam War lodged in our cultural memory.)

But I also think there is a value in asking what, if anything, Jarlath actually manages to accomplish through his rhetoric. And here, as with the *Phaedrus*, the lesson seems to me a cautionary one. It is hard to imagine Des and General reading Jarlath's convoluted and repetitive rhetoric with anything more than bafflement and perhaps thanks: *our crazy uncle has left us his money and this weird letter*. As works of literature, both texts are brilliant. As lessons in writing, both are failures. I suspect this is on purpose—that Plato and Dimock want us to notice how the lessons of their teachers begin to falter, to see the limits of their rhetorics. Socrates fails through his indifference to the actual views of the person he is talking with. Jarlath fails because he asks his method to do more than any method possibly can.

These are, of course, versions of the same problem. The more time you spend elaborating a general theory of writing, the less you have to give to the specific projects of individual writers. This is not to suggest that theory has no place in teaching writing. To the contrary. If a theme runs through the novels, movies, and plays I've looked at in this book, it's that theory gains its value in the act of teaching, of responding to student work. When Sassoon helps Owen revise the lines of "Anthem for Doomed Youth" in Pat Barker's *Regeneration*, he draws on a theory of poetry. When Frank pushes Rita to produce a more "considered essay" in *Educating Rita*, he relies on a theory of criticism. When teachers have no theory of writing, their work can be little more than a simple exercise in charisma, of dead poets and wonder boys seducing and inspiring their charges.

A good teacher needs to respond to a piece of writing with a sense of what it might become. To do so requires not only something like a rhetoric, a theory of writing, but also a close attentiveness to the aims of individual writers. We need to be willing, that is, to respond to one piece after another, each in its minute particulars, over and over again, to imagine that the next writer we read and work with might have something to say we haven't heard before, that their text might find a form that differs from what we've seen before. The measure of our work is what we help others to write.

Postscript

ON THE JOB

Whatever other problems they may face, fictional writing teachers tend to have enviable workloads. Most of the teachers in the books, movies, and plays I've looked at here appear to teach only one class—and that class is often quite small. Several work with just a single student writer. We encounter occasional hints of other classes or obligations, but those are placed well in the background. Our attention is focused on the work a teacher and student (or small group of students) do together.

While this strikes me as a reasonable plot device—especially for how it offers a novelist or dramatist the chance to draw not just teachers but students as complex characters—it also distorts the working experience of most of us who teach writing, which surely centers on the feeling of having much more to do than hours to do it in. No writing teacher comes home and wearily sighs, "I have a paper to correct this evening." It's always a stack, the latest set of fifteen or twenty or thirty or more pieces turned in by today's section or sections. I'd thus like to bring this study to a close by looking at a few books that make the working conditions of writing teachers a key element of their plots: Julie Schumacher's 2017 *Dear Committee Members*, Richard Russo's 1997 *Straight Man*, and James Hynes's 2001 *The Lecturer's Tale*.

None of these three books has anything of much interest to say about classroom teaching. But that's the point. They show how events conspire to make the already difficult work of teaching writing even harder to do well. They are campus novels rather than teaching novels, but all three books center on the work lives of ordinary academics at undistinguished institutions. They present academic life not as a calling or a form of minor

DOI: 10.7330/9781607329725.c006

celebrity but a job. And they show how the conditions of that job tend to work against good teaching.

I should also add that all three novels are very funny, accurate, and sharp in their depictions of college English departments. They are particularly good at documenting the sorts of nearly invisible tasks that can absorb much of an academic workday. For instance, Julie Schumacher's *Dear Committee Members* is an epistolary novel consisting of sixty-seven letters of recommendation written over the course of one academic year by Jay Fitger, a disgruntled professor of creative writing at Payne University, a fictional school of no particular distinction located somewhere in the Midwest. Jay's letters span the gamut. He recommends (in an often sideways manner) some students for fellowships and grad schools, other for jobs in paintball emporia, snack shops, and supermarkets. He writes on behalf of colleagues who are searching for jobs at other schools or who are looking for other positions at Payne. He supports still others for tenure, promotion, grants, awards, and chairs. It seems likely that most of his efforts do more harm than good. For while the first few of his references are merely cranky, Jay increasingly makes himself the focus of his letters. His recommendations become excruciatingly personal and ill-considered, filled with a venting of professional grudges and desperate attempts to rationalize his own mistakes and failures. And he has the added burden of needing to address several letters to either his ex-wife or his ex-lover, who are both also academics.

Jay's letters are intemperate and comic in a mean-spirited way. He writes double-edged praise like "intended to be philosophical rather than humorous, the story nevertheless succeeded to great comic effect" (138). But the sheer excess of detail in Jay's letters allows Schumacher to sketch a familiar portrait of a middling academic whose career is going nowhere. Payne University has frozen searches for new faculty in the liberal arts, and the English department has been placed in a kind of receivership with a sociologist serving as its temporary chair. The department offices are in a crumbling building under constant repair. (Jay's office is right beside the men's room.) And although he is a serious writer, Jay has promiscuously mined the details of his personal life for his fiction, to the detriment of both.

What is most striking, though, is how the novel performs its argument, showing us how Jay's energies as a novelist and teacher are displaced into the writing of recommendations that few people will ever read and even fewer will take seriously. As Jay observes in one of his early letters, in what is for him a modest digression:

> Though the academic year has just started I fear I am already losing the never-ending battle to catch up with the recommendations requested of me. Suffice it to say that the LOR has usurped the place of my own work, now adorned with cobwebs and dust in a remote corner of my office. (10–11)

It's soon made clear, though, that Jay has grown much less interested in finishing his "own work" than in the politics of literary and academic life—with who is appointed to direct what program, who is published by whom, who is offered what prize or residency. It's this undisguised self-absorption that gives *Dear Committee Members* its comic edge and allows Schumacher a chance to redeem Jay at its end. What I value most about her novel, though, is how it shows, in exaggerated form, how a minor if necessary task, the writing of recommendations, can crowd out the time and focus needed for the real work of teaching and writing.

Hank Devereaux Jr., the narrator and protagonist of Richard Russo's hilarious *Straight Man*, is yet another sad sack, although a more likable one than Jay Fitger. Hank is the son of a renowned literary theorist, William Henry Devereaux, Sr. As Hank tells us in the opening paragraphs of the novel, his well-published father favored "distinguished visiting professorships" with light teaching loads and the expectation "to read and think and write and publish and acknowledge in the preface of his next book the generosity of the institution that provided him the academic good life." Hank's mother, in contrast, "also an English professor, was hired as part of the package deal, to teach a full load and thereby help balance the books" (xii). The hierarchies of work in an English department were thus baked into the very structure of his boyhood family.

Hank has himself spent his career teaching a full load at the fictional West Central Pennsylvania University, an academic backwater in the rust belt of the state. It's the sort of place where ambition goes to die. Adhering to the conventions of the genre of the campus novel, Hank published a well-received first novel twenty years ago but has since settled more or less contentedly into coping with writer's block (or lethargy) and teaching section after section of creative writing and composition. I won't spoil the comic and convoluted plot of the novel with a summary, but it centers on Hank's shambolic attempts, as interim chair of the English department, to deal with a looming budget crisis. (One of his strategies involves threatening, while being interviewed for the local TV news, to kill one of the ducks on the campus pond each day the university budget is delayed.) Hank spends most of his time going from one quotidian meeting to the next—hiring, budget, retirement, and the like. He also teaches two classes. These are described only fleetingly in the novel and don't seem to occupy much of his attention. Teaching is only a part of his work week, not its center.

Hank's advanced fiction workshop has been stalled by a feud between the only two students in it who consider themselves serious writers: Solange, a wannabe poet, although "to her this has less to do with writing poetry than with adopting a superior attitude" (99), and Leo, an earnest boy with a Hemingway complex who, in his own words, "lives to write" (71) but unfortunately doesn't seem very good at it. The other students serve as an unnamed, frightened chorus. For his part, Hank seems unsuccessful in his attempts to convince Leo to "understate necrophilia" (97) in his stories or to get Solange to add some actions as well as metaphors to hers (349–50). It's a class running on autopilot.

His comp class goes even worse. Midway through the semester, Hank admits that "so far, I haven't persuaded my freshmen that the ability to persuade is an important skill" (200). So he starts winging it. On the spur of the moment, he assigns his students to write an essay persuading him to either (1) begin killing a duck a day, as he had threatened, theatrically, to do on the local TV news, or (2) not. Predictably, when the essays come due, most students argue for poultricide, as Hank learns to his dismay when he calls on several of them to read their pieces aloud in class. Desperate, Hank calls on his best writer, a quiet young woman named Blair, in the hope that she will somehow rescue the discussion, but in doing so he only manages to embarrass her (265–68). The class is a fiasco.

When we see Hank at other moments in the novel speaking with Leo, Solange, and Blair, it's clear that he's fond of each of them. He's a good guy at heart, just burned out and worn down, much like all the other middle-aged wonder boys in academic novels. That's not an excuse for indifferent teaching, but expectations are low and workloads high at West Central Pennsylvania U. What sets *Straight Man* apart from most academic novels is that at its end, Hank is neither lost nor redeemed. He doesn't start a new novel or resolve to become a better teacher. But the university weathers its fiscal crisis, as they almost always seem somehow to do, and Hank and his colleagues continue to trudge along pretty much as before, with a kind of collective, bemused shrug. The lessons of *Straight Man* have to do with finding happiness on the lower rungs of the academic ladder.

Still, for Hank and most of his colleagues, those rungs are pretty secure. They may be anonymous and overworked, but most of them hold tenure or the strong prospect of gaining it. They are solid members of the middle class. In contrast, *The Lecturer's Tale*, by James Hynes, fantasizes a revolt by the academic underclass. Or at least in part. *The Lecturer's Tale* is another difficult book to summarize. It has aspects of a David Lodge–like farce, with an array of flamboyant characters resembling well-known literary critics and theorists of the 1990s. It's also a gothic tale centering on an academic nobody, a visiting adjunct lecturer, who gains uncanny powers of persuasion. And it has elements of a realist, Richard Russo–like domestic comedy. It is a tour de force.

The lecturer of the tale, Nelson Humboldt, is about as unassuming as you can get, a young academic whose prospects are already declining. He holds a PhD from an undistinguished state university, with a dissertation on James Hogg, a forgotten literary figure. Basically, he likes to read. This makes him pretty much invisible to the clique of tenured theorists, feminists, neo-Marxists, and postcolonialists who run the English department at the prestigious Midwest University, where Nelson has bumbled into a job teaching three sections of composition and one of study skills each term. But even this small bit of luck runs out for him, as he is told in the opening pages of the novel that his contract will not be renewed at the end of the fall semester. In despair, he stumbles onto the Quad, only to have his index finger severed in a freak accident. After his finger is sewed back on at the hospital, Nelson discovers he can make others do his bidding simply by laying his hand gently upon them. His requests, at least at the start, are humble: a new contract to continue teaching composition, the friendship of his colleagues. But events unfold in increasingly madcap and outlandish ways, and the novel ends with the university almost literally turned upside down—with its famous library burned to the ground, the celebrity theorists fled from its faculty, a textbook publisher running its curriculum, and Nelson chairing the English department.

. But I get ahead of myself. One of the key moments in *The Lecturer's Tale* occurs early on, when Hynes describes Harbour Hall, where the English department is housed:

> There were nine floors . . . but only eight of them were above ground. During the fifties a windowless underground bunker had been sunk as a hideaway from nuclear war, with walls of reinforced concrete sixteen inches thick. The elevator sank below ground level and lurched to a stop . . . This was the portal to the Bomb Shelter, home of the Department of English's Composition Program. (62–63)

The theorists, of course, reside on the very top floor. Here below dwell the comp teachers, "the sad women in the basement," as the writing scholar Susan Miller once called them (1993, 121). Hynes goes several steps step further in a biting passage:

> Most of the comp teachers were divorced moms and single women with cats who taught eight classes a year and earned a thousand dollars per class, who clung to their semester-to-semester contracts with the desperate devotion of anchoresses. They combined the bitter esprit de corps of assembly-line workers with the literate work of the overeducated: They were the steerage of the English Department, the first to drown if the budget sprang a leak. They were the Morlocks to the Eloi of the eight floor . . . They were the colonial periphery, harvesting for pennies a day the department's raw material—undergraduates—and shipping these processed students farther up the hierarchy, thus creating the leisure for the professors at the imperial center to pursue their interests in feminist theory and postcolonial literature. (63)

This intellectual underworld is ruled by Linda Proserpina, MA, the director of composition, a chain-smoking wraith who has no more respect or affection for Nelson than do the theorists. Linda sees Nelson as an interloper, a dilettante with a literature PhD, almost a scab. He is someone who teaches comp not out of love but only because he has to.

And truth be told, Nelson seems an uninspired writing teacher. His one virtue is diligence. As his wife observes:

> She'd never completely understood the life of the young academic: why he taught four classes a semester for a fraction of the salary of professors who taught two, why he was never paid for the articles he published, why he stayed up to all hours of the night writing comments on the papers of students who would only throw them away after looking at the grade. (13)

Still, throughout the course of the novel, we never learn the name of a single undergraduate Nelson teaches. He views the textbook he has been given to use as offering "one part writing to two parts twelve-step program," and yet he's willing to assign projects from it like presentations on "My Most Important Personal Epiphany" (36). He is employed by a program in which only heroes and martyrs can thrive, and Nelson is neither. Four classes and an inane textbook have instead turned him into a drudge. He approaches his own writing much the same way: "Because he needed to publish and he didn't have any better ideas, Nelson ground out Hogg article after Hogg article" (33).

Like Hank in *Straight Man* but at a much earlier stage in his career, Nelson has been reduced to going through the motions. Hank and Nelson call to mind Ted Sizer's *Horace's Compromise* (1984). In this book, Sizer argues for restructuring the workloads of high school teachers so they can spend more time doing hands-on work with individual students. It's a sensible argument that got lost in the years of No Child Left Behind, Race to the Top, and the Common Core. At the center of the book is a composite character Sizer calls Horace Smith, a fifty-three-year-old English teacher, an "old pro" who loves his work and would never do anything else. And yet Horace has had to make a series of compromises simply to get through his workday. He rations the amount of time he devotes to preparing each class meeting, alternates the classes he collects homework from, assigns writing less often than he'd like (once a week rather than twice), restricts those writings to just a paragraph or two, and sometimes grades them using only a plus, check, or minus. As Sizer observes, "He hadn't time enough to do more" (16). He saves writing college recommendation letters for his Christmas vacation. And there are other activities that simply go by the wayside: revising curricula, meeting with parents, counseling students, reading in his field. These compromises gnaw at Horace. He is a professional who is not allowed the time or means to truly exercise his craft. Instead, he must find ways to work around "a chasm between the necessary and the provided" (21).

Straight Man is about living with a similar set of compromises. But *The Lecturer's Tale* ends with a fantasy of reform. When at the close of the novel Nelson improbably becomes English department chair, he decides to create a department "where pedagogy and scholarship are the same thing, where a good day in class is as exciting as another publication" (369). He thus appoints Linda Proserpina as assistant chair and promotes all of her composition instructors to professorships. Harbridge, the publishing company that now owns Midwest University, has standardized curricula through "strongly encouraging" the use of its own textbooks and instituting a stringent set of annual reviews for all instructors (376). But while most of the remaining university faculty chafe under this new system, the comp teachers find that their situation has improved:

> The corporate salary was actually better than the old university salary for comp teachers; year-to-year contracts were better than semester-to-semester, and Harbridge, mirabile dictu, actually provided benefits, sick days, and vacation time. To attract students, the classes were smaller, and Harbridge provided each instructor with brand-new copies of their entire textbook line. (376)

This is clearly a flawed utopia (as they all are). But the new, standardized Midwest U also reveals how the glamorous research university that came before it was a kind of Potemkin village, its facade of graduate seminars and advanced literature courses propped up by the labor of a teaching proletariat grinding out classes in composition for subsistence wages. The overall argument of the novel is not for regimentation but fairness.

As a case in point, the only star theorist who does not abandon Midwest University at the end of the novel is Anthony Pescecane, the regal ex-chair of the English department. Re-embracing his working-class New Jersey roots, Pescecane drops "Anthony" for "Tony," swaps his bespoke suits for jeans and muscle shirts, trades his Jaguar for a classic Mustang, and dives gladly into teaching composition to freshmen. Nelson is pleased but not fooled; he knows Pescecane has "a highly lucrative second career on the lecture circuit" (381), so he can afford to teach whatever and whomever he wants. But that's exactly the point. If it's to last, the comp revolution needs people like Tony Pescecane. Teaching writing shouldn't require a vow of poverty. A profession that demands the sacrifice of money and ambition will soon be left with only the saintly or desperate as its practitioners. The goal has to be not only to improve the lot of comp teachers but also to show how teaching writing can be a welcome part of a successful professorial career—a task for Tony Pescecane as well as Nelson Humboldt and Linda Proserpina.

The Lecturer's Tale closes with Nelson entering his classroom on the first day of a new semester. For the first time in a longish

novel, we are offered an extended description of the undergraduates he teaches:

> Some of them were sullen, some bright-eyed, most of them wary.
> The former University of the Midwest had finally achieved the
> diversity to which it had long paid lip service; Nelson no longer
> faced the overindulged, pampered, narcissistic, upper-middle-
> class white kids who used to make up the university's student
> body. Now he faced the kids who couldn't have afforded it or met
> its entrance requirements before: inner-city black kids, Latino
> kids from farmworker families, poor white kids from dying indus-
> trial towns, divorced moms, downsized middle-managers, laid-off
> factory workers . . . Taken as a whole, they were both ill prepared
> and heartbreakingly expectant. (384–85)

When Nelson looks out at this group, he wonders what he has
to offer them. Is what they really need a chance to read some
books and to try to formulate their own ideas about them? "It
will have to do, he told himself, because it's all I've got to give
them" (386). It's a wonderful moment, both humbling and
inspiring, as a teacher begins to speak not from a sense of mastery but from doubt and an anxious desire to help. That's what
drives the work of the best writing teachers we see in fiction,
drama, and film: an urge to connect, to work together on a text,
to imagine new possibilities for writing.

BACKGROUND READINGS

INTRODUCTION

In doing the research for this book, I was buoyed by the discovery of a few fellow spirits who have also looked to literature and film for insights into teaching writing. Although she is more interested than I am in the personal (and sometimes erotic) relationships between teachers and students, Jo Keroes's 1999 *Tales Out of School* stands out as a book-length study that takes what non-academics have to say about teaching seriously. Similarly, in "Fear of Narrative" (2007), Brian Schwartz looks at how two short stories hint at the personal reasons that lead two very different composition teachers to focus on matters of either correctness or expression. Such fiction, Schwartz suggests, can tell us something about how lived experience shapes and informs our approaches to teaching. More recently, in his 2018 "Whether Wit or Wisdom," Paul T. Corrigan makes the case for approaching literary texts as "parables of teaching: rich, rough, perceptive accounts of what it means to teach and how to teach more effectively."

However, most writing by academics on how popular texts have represented teachers has been far more negative and critical. The more openly political critiques follow the lead of the Frankfurt School in viewing most forms of education as indoctrination. Cultural critics like William Ayers (1994) and Henry Giroux (2002) argue that heroic depictions of teachers in film reinforce an ethic of individualism by glossing over the systemic injustices that deny many students a chance at a good education. Teacher-heroes on film and TV, they argue, are far more often shown as helping kids make it within the system than urging them to resist its inequalities. Rebecca Brittenham (2005) offers a pithy synopsis of this line of thought in "Goodbye,

DOI: 10.7330/9781607329725.c007

Mr. Hip," an essay on how television has presented sanitized versions of "radical" teachers.

Feminist scholars like Dale M. Bauer (1998) and Mary M. Dalton (1999) have extended this critique by showing how Hollywood depictions of women teachers tend to eroticize and trivialize them as either nurturers or sexpots. Dalton has twice updated her comprehensive study of teachers in film, *The Hollywood Curriculum* (1999, 2010, 2017), and has also coauthored, with Laura R. Linder, another similarly exhaustive study of *Teacher TV* (2008). Both volumes document how media depictions of teachers continually recycle stereotypes about race and gender. In his 2011 *Dead from the Waist Down*, A. D. Nuttall adds support to this critique by showing how intellectuals of both sexes are commonly shown as brittle and sexless creatures.

The tone of writing about the academic or college novel, however, has been more varied. The baseline study here is John Lyons's 1962 *The College Novel in America*, updated in 1974. It's a peculiar book, with no real argument of its own. Rather, Lyons offers a series of pocket reviews, one after the other, of 216 American novels set on college campuses, beginning with Hawthorne's *Fanshawe* and ending with works by Malamud and Roth. He offers a number of useful insights into particular novels. What's odd, though, is his tone, which is dismissive throughout. He begins by noting the "general lack of excellence" (xiii) of the works he is considering and concludes by noting that "it may seem unfair to carp at the lack of distinction in the novels about academic life" (186). And yet included on his list are several of the greatest American novels of the twentieth century, including Willa Cather's *The Professor's House* (1925), Mary McCarthy's *The Groves of Academe* (1952), Randall Jarrell's *Pictures from an Institution* (1954), and Vladimir Nabokov's *Pnin* (1957).

More fun than Lyons, if perhaps even more eccentric, is John Kramer's *The American College Novel: An Annotated Bibliography*. The 648 items in the second edition of this volume (2003), which is divided into Student-Centered and Staff-Centered novels, are given pointed and lively annotations. I was particularly taken by Kramer's tongue-in-cheek observation, explaining the structure of his book: "Of course, as sometimes happens in the real world of higher education as well, fictional faculty members and administrators occasionally intrude into the lives of fictional students, and fictional students sometimes appear in the worlds of fictional faculty and administrators" (ix). My own concern here has been with those occasional intrusions and appearances.

Elaine Showalter offers an appreciative and cosmopolitan take on "novels about professors" (7) in her 2005 *Faculty Towers*. Her book is essentially a fan's guide to the academic novel as an escapist genre. In a perceptive 2012 essay titled "The Rise of the Academic Novel," Jeffrey J. Williams offers yet another update. Williams distinguishes between what he calls "campus novels" (which focus on students) and "academic" ones (which center on professors). He then argues that in recent years the academic novel—which he views as offering midlife "anxiety narratives"— has largely superseded the campus one. However, like Lyons and Showalter, he does not point to many novels in which teachers and students actually interact. That topic, to borrow a phrase from perhaps the most famous of all campus novels, Kingsley Amis's *Lucky Jim* (1954), remains "strangely neglected."

CHAPTER 1: DEAD POETS AND WONDER BOYS

Academic critics of *Dead Poets Society* begin again with Ayers (1994) and Giroux (2002). The basic argument is that the romantic individualism advocated by the film tends to prop up more than subvert the social status quo. Similar criticisms of the movie have been leveled by Keith Barton (2006), Mark Collins (1989), Kenneth Dettmar (2014), Robert Heilman (1991), and Sally Robinson (2000). Steve Benton joins this chorus of criticism in his fine 2008 dissertation, "Ichabod's Children: Anti-Intellectualism and the American Pedagogical Imagination," but also notes that the critics of *Dead Poets Society* tend, ironically, to take on Keating-like roles themselves as intellectual crusaders.

In *Tales Out of School,* Jo Keroes offers an appreciative reading of *Educating Rita* as a teacher-student romance that ends in a meeting of minds rather than bodies. Richard E. Miller is less impressed, arguing instead in his 2005 *Writing at the End of the World* that the film condescends toward Rita as it frets over whether she will lose her authentic voice through the process of education (165–66). Similarly, Deanne Bogdan, in a perceptive essay on "Pygmalion as Pedagogue" (1984), suggests that Frank "perceives Rita through a dark glass of his own insecurities and a sentimentalized view of literary education" (68).

CHAPTER 2: BEGINNINGS

When David Mamet's *Oleanna* was first performed in 1992, it was widely understood as his response to the debates over sexual harassment brought to light by the Clarence Thomas–Anita Hill hearings—an interpretation Mamet himself encouraged (see Weber 1992). The exact aim of this response, however, was less clear—as can be seen in a *New York Times* roundtable in which six viewers offer highly divergent readings of the sexual politics of the play (Brownmuller et al. 1992). Reviewers in the mainstream press also disagreed: Frank Rich (1992) praised Mamet's unwillingness to "pander" in the *New York Times,* while in the *Times Literary Supplement* Elaine Showalter (1992) accused him of stacking the deck against Carol.

But by 1998, critics like Richard Badenhausen were arguing that "the message of *Oleanna* appears to have much less to do with political correctness and sexual harassment and more to do with the difficulties of acquiring and controlling language" (1–2). For Badenhausen, this means that the play is more concerned with power than sex, and he goes on to offer a trenchant criticism of John's failures as a teacher, most of which have to do with his unwillingness to actually listen and respond to Carol. Stanton Garner (2000) and Christine Macleod (1995) also offer similar takes on the play, although without Badenhausen's fine-tuned attention to the micropolitics of teaching.

In his introduction to the 2006 print version of *The History Boys*, Alan Bennett writes that the play is about the "two sorts of teaching" exemplified by Hector and Irwin. But he offers a more nuanced understanding of teaching in a 2004 interview with Nicholas Hytner, in which he grants that if his play offers any sort of model of good teaching, it also involves Lintott's emphasis on getting the facts straight. John Stinson endorses this tripartite view of teaching in his 2006 analysis of the play while also noting what remains the case more than a decade later, which is that while *The History Boys* has received popular acclaim as both a play and a film, its subtle take on teaching has not received much notice from academic critics. The few exceptions are cranky and defensive: a 2006 piece by Warren Goldstein lamenting Bennett's treatment of the discipline of history and a 2006 essay by Martin Jacobi criticizing his view of classical education.

A similar pattern of popular acclaim and critical indifference holds for *Push* and *Up the Down Staircase*. Most scholars who have written about *Push* have been drawn, reasonably, to its accounts of racial injustice and sexual abuse, as well as to Precious's heroic attempts to resist them. Sika Dagbovie-Mullins summarizes what research has been done on the novel in her 2011 article "From Living to Eat to Writing to Live," in which she analyzes Precious's uses of writing to form a sense of self and agency. Laurie Stapleton (2004) also focuses on the ways Sapphire highlights and honors the writing and voice of Precious, as does Gayle Pemberton in her admiring 1996 review of the novel. Both Stapleton and Pemberton also briefly note Blue Rain's imaginative and radical work as a teacher, but the classroom scenes and student writings that make up so much of the novel are not offered close analysis by any critic I've come across. Still, though, the attention given to *Push* exceeds that which academics have paid to the popular, wise, and formally experimental *Up the Down Staircase*—which has been none at all.

CHAPTER 3: WORK IN PROGRESS

Mustang Sally, Blue Angel, and *All Is Forgotten, Nothing Is Lost* were all reviewed warmly in the mainstream press (see, for instance, Slade 1992; Sage 2000; Wineapple 2010), but none of them has received much attention from academic critics. With the novels of William Coles, this pattern of popular approval and academic indifference is turned upside down. I've been unable to find a review of Coles's work in the popular press. But he was for many years a prominent figure in the teaching of academic writing, and both *The Plural I* and *Seeing through Writing* have been closely analyzed by other composition teachers. Indeed, the first academic article I published, in 1987, was on *The Plural I.* My view of the book at the time was more admiring. Kim Flachman (1989), Bruce Horner (1994), and Peter Wayne Moe (2018) have also written perceptive analyses of *The Plural I* and *Seeing through Writing.* And in *Fencing with Words* (1996), Robin Varnum offers a detailed study of the manly, push-and-shove tradition of teaching writing at Amherst College, the backdrop for Alison Lurie's *Love and Friendship* and the place where Coles forged his approach as a teacher.

Pat Barker's *Regeneration* is one of the towering British novels of the twentieth century and as such has been the focus of much analysis. But while critics have often commented on the scenes involving Sassoon and Owen, they have seldom read their relationship as that of teacher and student. And so, for example, in a perceptive piece titled "Regenerating Wilfred Owen" (2009), Kaley Joyes shows how the experience of watching Sassoon help Owen develop and revise "Anthem for Doomed Youth" changes our view of the poem, helping us to see it as a crafted response to war rather than an immediate outburst. But she does not comment on how Sassoon contributes as a teacher to that process of crafting. Responses to Skármeta's *The Postman* have been similar—Mario and Neruda tend to be viewed as unlikely friends and collaborators rather than as teacher and student. Ethan Bumas (1993), however, does recognize *The Postman* as in some ways about teaching and writes a sensitive, detailed appreciation of the relationship between Neruda and Mario, arguing that in Skármeta's novel, "writing . . . is a group project" (17). Indeed, this may point to the key insight into teaching offered by both novels—that at its best, teaching is a form not of seduction but of friendship and collaboration.

CHAPTER 4: FORGING A SELF

In his 2008 dissertation, "Mentor-Teaching in the English Classroom," Timothy Blue discusses several of the texts I look at in this book. He offers a much less sympathetic reading of Ms. Moray in *Prep* than I do, viewing her missteps with Lee as signs of authoritarian overreaching more than anxiety. His view of Frank in *Educating Rita* is similarly unforgiving. In her 2014 "Between Meritocracy and the Old Boy Network," Sophie Spieler reads *Prep* as a kind of parable of cultural capital, with Lee Fiora struggling to acquire a social standing that all of her classmates already possess.

Francine Prose's *Blue Angel* was well received by academic critics as a nuanced updating of the campus novel. William G. Tierney (2002), for instance, lauds Prose for presenting Ted Swenson as someone who makes many of the predictable mistakes of middle age but who also learns, painfully, from doing so. Jesse Kavadlo discusses both *Mustang Sally* and *Blue Angel* in his 2004 "Blue Angels Meet Dying Animals," but his interest lies entirely in the two novels as critiques of political correctness—which actually strikes me as the salient weakness of both books. In contrast, in her brief 2000 review of the novel, Gail Pool singles out its classroom scenes, noting sympathetically that "as the students critique each hopeless story, suggesting an alternation here, a new ending there, trying to perform 'the weekly miracle of healing the terminally ill with cosmetic surgery,' their comments bring them and the novel's issues—of gender, political correctness, education, ambition, and talent—to life" (32). Here Pool emphasizes what Proses's character Ted Swanson has forgotten—that the goal of a writing class can go beyond the simple nurturing of talent.

I was surprised to discover that May Sarton's *The Small Room* was published to tepid or hostile reviews from academic critics, who tend to dismiss it for pretty much the same reasons I value it. Anne Halley (1961) suggested that the novel was too full of what are "at best matters for a teachers' seminar" (192–93), while Kenneth E. Eble (1962) and Frederick S. Kiley (1962) criticized the smallness not only of Sarton's setting but of her ambitions as a writer. Eble faults her "brisk, prim, and stock handling of a small situation" (115); Kiley disdainfully claims that "the book hardly enlists sympathies from the inhabitants of the enormous room some men [*sic*] call life" (508). Later readers of the novel have been less masculinist and more sympathetic. In her 1983 "Faculty Images in Recent Fiction," Frances K. Barasch dismissed the usual protagonists of the academic novel as "white, male neurotics, oversexed, under-appreciated and probably Jewish" (28), arguing that women novelists like Sarton, Alison Lurie, and Mary McCarthy have offered more fine-grained portraits of academic life. Writing at much the same time, Linda Robertson (1982) pointed to Lucy Winter as an example of the sort of college teacher who might profit from a faculty workshop on designing writing assignments! And in 1997, Michael Katz invoked *The Small Room* as an example of the usefulness of looking to fiction for insights into the situational and emotional undercurrents of teaching that more conventional research often fails to offer. Nancy Porter anticipated this view in her lovely 1994 appreciation of Sarton's novel as offering an unusual (and much-needed) image of a happy and successful woman teacher. And in 2004, William G. Tierney singled out the seriousness of Sarton's approach as a valuable contrast to what he sees as the ironic nihilism of most recent academic novels.

Tobias Wolff's *Old School*, in contrast, was published to glowing reviews in the popular press (see, for examples, Ciarruru 2003; Morrisson 2004; Scott 2003) but has so far received scant notice from academics. To date, the scholars who've written about the novel have largely focused on the relationships between it and Wolff's better-known autobiographical writings. See, for example, David Gooblar's "Tobias Wolff's *Old School*: Truth, Lies, Fiction, and the American Boarding School" (2014).

CHAPTER 5: THE LIMITS OF RHETORIC

Two books provide a powerful context for reading Marilyn Sternglass's *Time to Know Them*. The first is *Errors and Expectations* (1979) by Mina P. Shaughnessy, who served as the director of basic writing at City College during the first years of open admissions in the 1970s. Her book is a powerful testament to the potential of students who have been disserved by their previous schooling. The other book is *City on a Hill* (1994), a tendentious argument by the journalist James Traub for dismantling the basic writing program Shaughnessy created. His aim is to defend academic standards and cut expenses at the possible (if not probable) cost of limiting the hopes of many adult and working students to gain access to the four-year college system. Sternglass is interviewed several times by Traub.

Jacques Derrida offers a famous (and famously difficult) analysis of the shifting relationships between speech and writing in the *Phaedrus*, in his essay "Plato's Pharmacy," published in *Disseminations* (1983). Jasper Neel offers a lucid account of these arguments in his 1988 *Plato, Derrida, and Writing*. The *Rhetorica ad Herennium*, which Jarlath compulsively rewrites in *A Short Rhetoric*, remains as arcane and unreadable as ever. But if you must, there is the classic 1954 Loeb edition translated by Harry Caplan.

Peter Dimock's *A Short Rhetoric for Leaving the Family* has been overlooked by both popular and academic critics. I have found only a small handful of trade notices and an unperceptive 1999 review by David Beard in *Rhetoric Review*. Beard is disappointed that Jarlath is not a better rhetorical theorist—which seems to me to miss the point of the novel. Dimock's book should be better known, both as an innovative fiction and for what it suggests about teaching.

POSTSCRIPT: ON THE JOB

Jeanne Marie Rose also reads *Straight Man* and *The Lecturer's Tale* as comments on working conditions in English departments in her perceptive piece "Managing Writing: Composition in the Academic Novel" (2009). Her view of the two novels is less approving than mine, largely because of her annoyance with how both Russo and Hynes routinely disparage composition as an intellectual field even as they express sympathy for individual writing teachers. She's right—although I'd also argue that neither novel offers much respect for scholars or teachers of literature either. Other academic critics have read *Straight Man* as offering lessons in collegiality, if only through negative example. See Dennis Baron's "Avoiding the Role of Straight Man" (2004) and Lynn Z. Bloom's "Collegiality, the Game" (2005). Most academic readers of *The Lecturer's Tale* have focused on Hynes's comic and accurate send-up of literary theory and celebrity. See, for instance, Sanford Pinsker (2003) and Dale Bailey and Jack Slay Jr. (2003). Julie Schumacher's *Dear Committee Members* garnered brief and enthusiastic reviews from the *New Yorker* (Waldman 2018), NPR (Corrigan 2014), and the *New York Times* (Clark 2014) but has not yet received much academic commentary.

In his 2004 essay "Academic Freedom and Tenure: Between Fiction and Reality," William G. Tierney offers a comprehensive and stinging review of the way tenure has been depicted in academic novels. He argues that novelists have shifted from presenting tenure as a guarantee of intellectual freedom to satirizing it as a cover for "academic politics and sexual hijinks" (175). A result is that "in virtually all novels, teaching is not only unimportant, it is irrelevant. Students are treated as objects, if they are discussed at all, and faculty receive little, if any, delight in teaching" (172). While I'm sure it's clear by now that I agree on the whole with this gloomy assessment, my aim in this book has also been to point to some hopeful exceptions to Tierney's rule.

REFERENCES

Allen, Edward. 1992. *Mustang Sally*. New York: Norton.

Amis, Kingsley. 2012 [1954]. *Lucky Jim*. New York: Penguin.

Asquith, Anthony, dir. 1951. *The Browning Version*. Javelin. Film.

Ayers, William. 1994. "A Teacher Ain't Nothin' But a Hero." In *Images of Schoolteachers in Twentieth-Century America*, ed. Pamela Bolotin Joseph and Gail E. Burnaford. New York: St. Martin's, 147–56.

Badenhausen, Richard. 1998. "The Modern Academy Raging in the Dark: Misreading Mamet's Political Incorrectness in *Oleanna*." *College Literature* 25: 1–19.

Bailey, Dale, and Jack Slay Jr. 2003. "A Counterhegemonic World: James Hynes' Tales of Academic Horror." *Studies in Popular Culture* 25: 25–32.

Barasch, Frances K. 1983. "Faculty Images in Recent Fiction." *College Literature* 10: 28–37.

Barker, Pat. 1992. *Regeneration*. New York: Dutton.

Baron, Dennis. 2004. "Avoiding the Role of Straight Man." *Chronicle of Higher Education* (June 18): C1.

Bartholomae, David. 1985. "Inventing the University." In *When A Writer Can't Write: Studies in Writer's Block and Other Composing Problems*, ed. Mike Rose. New York: Guilford, 134–65.

Barton, Keith C. 2006. "After the Essays Are Ripped Out, What? The Limits of a Reflexive Encounter." *Counterpoints* 272: 241–44.

Bauer, Dale M. 1998. "Indecent Proposals: Teachers in the Movies." *College English* 60, no. 3 (March): 301–17.

Beard, David. 1999. "Review of *A Short Rhetoric for Leaving the Family*." *Rhetoric Review* 18: 215–18.

Bennett, Alan. 2006. *The History Boys*. New York: Faber.

Benton, Steve. 2008. "Ichabod's Children: Anti-Intellectualism and the American Pedagogical Imagination." PhD dissertation, University of Illinois at Chicago.

Bloom, Lynn Z. 2005. "Collegiality, the Game." *Symploke* 13: 207–18.

Blue, Timothy. 2008. "Mentor-Teaching in the English Classroom." PhD dissertation, Georgia State University, Atlanta.

Bogdan, Deanne. 1984. "Pygmalion as Pedagogue: Subjectivist Bias in the Teaching of Literature." *English Education* 16: 67–75.

Braithwaite, E. R. 1959. *To Sir, with Love*. New York: Prentice Hall.

Brittenham, Rebecca. 2005. "Goodbye, Mr. Hip." *College English* 68: 149–67.

Brooks, Richard, dir. 1955. *The Blackboard Jungle*. MGM. Film.

Brown, Jayne Relaford. 2000. "Emily Dickinson Attends a Writing Workshop." In *Visiting Emily: Poems Inspired by the Life and Works of Emily Dickinson*, ed. Sharon Cogil and Thom Tamarro. Des Moines: University of Iowa Press, 8.

Brownmiller, Susan, Enrique Fernandez, Deborah Tannen, Mark Alan Stamaty, Ellen Schwartzman, and Lionel Tiger. 1992. "He Said . . . She Said . . . Who Did What?" *New York Times* (November 15), Section 2, 6.

DOI: 10.7330/9781607329725.c008

Bumas, Ethan Shaskan. 1993. "Metaphor's Exile: The Poets and Postmen of Antonio Skármeta." *Latin American Literary Review* 21: 9–20.

Chang, Lan Samantha. 2010. *All Is Forgotten, Nothing Is Lost.* New York: Norton.

Ciarruru, Carmela. 2003. "Lessons Learned in *Old School.*" *Los Angeles Times* (December 10).

Clark, Brock. 2014. "Comic Novels." *New York Times* (October 31).

Clavell, James, dir. 1967. *To Sir, with Love.* Columbia. Film.

Coles, William E., Jr. 1978. *The Plural I: The Teaching of Writing.* New York: Holt.

Coles, William E., Jr. 1988. *Seeing through Writing.* New York: HarperCollins.

Collins, Mark. 1989. "Make-Believe in *Dead Poets Society.*" *English Journal* 78: 74–75.

Corrigan, Maureen. 2014. "In a Funny New Novel, a Professor Writes to *Dear Committee Members.*" *Fresh Air,* NPR (August 12).

Corrigan, Paul T. 2018. "Whether Wit or Wisdom: Resisting the Decline of the Humanities from Within." *Profession: Archive* (March). https://profession.mla .org/whether-wit-or-wisdom-resisting-the-decline-of-the-humanities-from -within/.

Cross, Amanda. 1981. *Death in a Tenured Position.* New York: Ballantine.

Dagbovie-Mullins, Sika. 2011. "From Living to Eat to Writing to Live: Metaphors of Consumption and Production in Sapphire's *Push.*" *African American Review* 44: 435–52.

Dalton, Mary M. 1999, 2010, 2017. *The Hollywood Curriculum: Teachers and Teaching in the Movies.* New York: Lang.

Dalton, Mary M., and Laura R. Linder. 2008. *Teacher TV: Sixty Years of Teachers on Television.* New York: Lang.

Daniels. Lee, dir. 2009. *Precious.* Lionsgate. Film.

Daspit, Toby, and John A. Weaver, eds. 1999. *Popular Culture and Critical Pedagogy: Reading, Constructing, Connecting.* New York: Garland.

Derrida, Jacques. 1983. *Disseminations.* Trans. Barbara Johnson. Chicago: University of Chicago Press.

Dettmar, Kevin J.H. 2014. "*Dead Poets Society* Is a Terrible Defense of the Humanities." *The Atlantic* (February 19). https://www.theatlantic.com/edu cation/archive/2014/02/-em-dead-poets-society-em-is-a-terrible-defense-of -the-humanities/283853/.

Dimock, Peter. 1990. *A Short Rhetoric for Leaving the Family.* Mclean, IL: Dalkey Archive Press.

Eble, Kenneth E. 1962. "Review of *The Small Room.*" *Journal of Higher Education* 33: 115.

Edson, Margaret. 1999. *Wit.* New York: Faber.

Figgis, Mike, dir. 1994. *The Browning Version.* Paramount. Film.

Fish, Stanley. 1990. *Doing What Comes Naturally: Change, Rhetoric, and the Practice of Theory in Literary and Legal Studies.* Durham, NC: Duke University Press.

Flachman, Kim. 1989. "Review of *The Plural I* and *Seeing through Writing.*" *CCC* 40: 357–60.

Garner, Stanton. 2000. "Framing the Classroom: Pedagogy, Power, *Oleanna.*" *Theatre Topics* 10: 39–52.

Gilbert, Lewis, dir. 1983. *Educating Rita.* Columbia. Film.

Giroux, Henry. 2002. *Breaking into the Movies: Film and the Culture of Politics.* Malden, MA: Blackwell.

Goldstein, Warren. 2006. "On the Stage, History Belittled." *Chronicle of Higher Education* (September 1): B11.

Gooblar, David. 2014. "Tobias Wolff's *Old School*: Truth, Lies, Fiction, and the American Boarding School." *Critique: Studies in Contemporary Fiction* 55: 358–72.

Gruwell, Erin, and the Freedom Writers. 2007. *The Freedom Writers Diary*. New York: Random.

Halley, Anne. 1961. "The Good Life in Recent Fiction." *Massachusetts Review* 3: 190–96.

Hanson, Curtis, dir. 2000. *Wonder Boys*. Paramount. Film.

Harris, Joseph. 1987. "The Plural Text/The Plural Self: Roland Barthes and William Coles." *College English* 49: 158–70.

Heilman, Robert B. 1991. "The Great-Teacher Myth." *American Scholar* 60: 417–23.

Herek, Stephen, dir. 1995. *Mr. Holland's Opus*. Buena Vista. Film.

Hilton, James. 1934. *Goodbye, Mr. Chips*. New York: Bantam.

Hoffman, Michael, dir. 2002. *Emperor's Club*. Beacon. Film.

Horner, Bruce. 1994. "Resisting Traditions in Composing Composition." *JAC* 14: 495–519.

Hynes, James. 2001. *The Lecturer's Tale*. New York: Picador.

Hytner, Nicholas. 2004. "The Truth behind *The History Boys*." *Telegraph* (June 21). https://www.telegraph.co.uk/culture/theatre/drama/3619379/The-truth -behind-the-History-Boys.html.

Hytner, Nicholas, dir. 2006. *The History Boys*. Columbia. Film.

"Introduction to Film." 2009. *Community*, Episode 3, Season 1. NBC (October 1).

Jacobi, Martin. 2006. "The Sad Reception of Classical Education in Alan Bennett's *The History Boys*." *South Atlantic Review* 71: 76–99.

Joyes, Kaley. 2009. "Regenerating Wilfrid Owen: Pat Barker's *Revisions*." *Mosaic* 42: 169–83.

Kael, Pauline. 1989. "*Dead Poets Society*: Stonework." *New Yorker* (June 26): 70–71.

Katz, Michael. 1997. "On Becoming a Teacher: May Sarton's *A Small Room*." *Philosophy of Education 1997*, ed. Susan Laird, 214–22. Urbana: University of Illinois.

Kaufman, Bel. 1962. "From a Teacher's Wastebasket." *Saturday Review* (November 17): 58–61.

Kaufman, Bel. 1964. *Up the Down Staircase*. New York: Harper.

Kaufman, Stanley. 1989. "Review of *Dead Poets Society*." *New Republic* 200 (June 26): 26.

Kavadlo, Jesse. 2004. "Blue Angels Meet Dying Animals: Textual and Sexual Subversion in the Clinton-Era Academic Novel." *Journal of the Midwest Language Association* 37: 11–25.

Keroes, Jo. 1999. *Tales out of School: Gender, Longing, and the Teacher in Fiction and Film*. Carbondale: Southern Illinois University Press.

Kiley, Frederick S. 1962. "Halls of Ivy." *Clearing House* 36: 508.

King, Stephen. 1988. *Misery*. New York: Signet.

Kramer, John. 2004. *The American College Novel: An Annotated Bibliography*. 2nd ed. Lanham, MD: Scarecrow.

Lagravenese, Richard, dir. 2007. *Freedom Writers*. Paramount. Film.

Levine, Richard, dir. 2017. *Submission*. Front Row Entertainment. Film.

Lodge, David. 1985. *Small World*. New York: Penguin.

Lurie, Alison. 1962. *Love and Friendship*. New York: Holt.

Lyons, John. 1962. *The College Novel in America*. Carbondale: Southern Illinois University Press.

Lyons, John. 1974. "The College Novel in America: 1962–74." *Critique: Studies in Contemporary Fiction* 16: 121–28.

Macleod, Christine. 1995. "The Politics of Gender, Language, and Hierarchy in Mamet's *Oleanna*." *Journal of American Studies* 29: 199–213.

Mamet, David. 1993. *Oleanna*. New York: Vintage.

Mamet, David, dir. 1994. *Oleanna*. Film.

McCarthy, Mary. 1952. *The Groves of Academe*. New York: Harcourt.

Miller, Richard E. 2005. *Writing at the End of the World*. Pittsburgh: University of Pittsburgh Press.

Miller, Susan. 1993. *Textual Carnivals: The Politics of Composition*. Carbondale: Southern Illinois University Press.

Moe, Peter Wayne. 2018. "Reading Coles Reading Themes: Epideictic Rhetoric and the Teaching of Writing." *CCC* 69: 433–57.

Morrison, Blake. 2004. "A Class Apart." *The Guardian* (January 23): 23.

Mulligan, Robert, dir. 1967. *Up the Down Staircase*. Warner. Film.

Neame, Robert, dir. 1968. *The Prime of Miss Jean Brodie*. Twentieth Century Fox. Film.

Neel, Jasper. 1988. *Plato, Derrida, and Writing*. Carbondale: Southern Illinois University Press.

Newell, Mike, dir. 2003. *Mona Lisa Smile*. Revolution Studios. Film.

Nuttall, A. D. 2011. *Dead from the Waist Down: Scholars and Scholarship in Literature and the Popular Imagination*. New Haven, CT: Yale University Press.

Owen, Cliff, dir. 1958. *The Browning Version*. ITV Playhouse. Film.

Owen, Wilfred. 1917. "Anthem for Dead Youth." Manuscript with comments by Siegfried Sassoon. *British Library: The Poetry Manuscripts of Wilfred Owen*. https://www.bl.uk/collection-items/the-poetry-manuscripts-of-wilfred-owen.

Pakula, Alan J., dir. 1979. *Starting Over*. Paramount. Film.

Papa, Lee. 2004. "Mamet's Oleanna in Context: Performance, Personal, Pedagogy." In *Imagining the Academy; Higher Education and Popular Culture*, ed. Susan Edgerton, Gunilla Holm, Toby Daspit, and Paul Farber, New York: Routledge, 217–29.

Pemberton, Gayle. 1996. "A Hunger for Language." *Women's Review of Books* 14, no. 2 (November): 1–2.

Pinsker, Sanford. 2003. "Postmodern Theory and the Academic Novel's Latest Turn." *Sewanee Review* 111: 183–91.

Plato. 1995. *Phaedrus*. Trans. Alexander Nehamas and Paul Woodruff. Indianapolis: Hackett.

Polan, Dana. 1996. "The Professors of History." In *The Persistence of History*, ed. Vivian Sobchack. New York: Routledge, 235–56.

Pool, Gail. 2000. "Lower Education." *Women's Review of Books* 17 (July): 32.

Porter, Nancy. 1994. "Female Faculty: Realities and Representations." *Women's Studies Quarterly* 22: 35–41.

Prose, Francine. 2000. *Blue Angel.* New York: HarperCollins.

Radford, Michael, dir. 1995. *Il Postino.* Miramax. Film.

Rattigan, Terrence. 1948, 2008. *The Browning Version.* London: Nick Hern Books.

Rebeck, Theresa. 2012. *Seminar.* Portland, ME: Smith and Kraus.

Reiner, Rob, dir. 1990. *Misery.* Castlerock. Film.

Rhetorica ad Herennium. 1954. Trans. Harry Caplan. Cambridge: Harvard University Press.

Rich, Frank. 1992. "Oleanna; Mamet's New Play Detonates the Fury of Sexual Harassment." *New York Times* (October 26), C11.

Richards, I. A. 1924, 2001. *Principles of Literary Criticism.* New York: Routledge.

Richards, I. A. 1942. *How to Read a Page.* New York: Norton.

Robertson, Linda R. 1982. "Assignments in the Humanities: Writing Intensive Course Design." *JAC* 3: 48–59.

Robinson, Sally. 2000. *Marked Men: White Masculinity in Crisis.* New York: Columbia University Press.

Rose, Jeanne Marie. 2009. "Managing Writing: Composition in the Academic Novel." *Modern Language Studies* 39: 56–65.

Russell, Willy. 1980, 2009. *Educating Rita.* London: Methuen.

Russo, Richard. 1997. *Straight Man.* New York: Random.

Sage, Lorna. 2000. "Pictures from a Politically Correct Institution." *New York Times* (April 16).

Sapphire. 1996. *Push: A Novel.* New York: Knopf.

Sarton, May. 1961. *The Small Room.* New York: Norton.

Schumacher, Julie. 2015. *Dear Committee Members.* New York: Anchor.

Schwartz, J. Brian. 2007. "Fear of Narrative: Revisiting the Bartholomae-Elbow Debate through the Figure of the Writing Teacher in Contemporary American Fiction." *Rhetoric Review* 26, no. 4: 425–39.

Scott, A. O. 2003. "Famous Writers School." *New York Times* (November 23).

Shaughnessy, Mina P. 1979. *Errors and Expectations: A Guide for the Teacher of Basic Writing.* New York: Oxford University Press.

Shelton, Ron, dir. 1988. *Bull Durham.* Mount. Film.

Showalter, Elaine. 1992. "Acts of Violence: David Mamet and the Language of Men." *Times Literary Supplement* (November 6): 16.

Showalter, Elaine. 2005. *Faculty Towers: The Academic Novel and Its Discontents.* Philadelphia: University of Pennsylvania Press.

Simpson, Michael A., dir. 1985. *The Browning Version.* BBC. Film.

Sittenfeld, Curtis. 2005. *Prep.* New York: Random.

Sizer, Theodore. 1984. *Horace's Compromise: The Dilemma of the American High School.* Boston: Houghton.

Skármeta, Antonio. 1985, 1995. *The Postman.* Trans. Katherine Silver. New York: Pantheon.

Slade, George. 1992. "Go Vegan or Die!" *New York Times* (December 13).

Solondz, Todd J., dir. 2001. *Storytelling.* New Line. Film.

Spark, Muriel. 1962. *The Prime of Miss Jean Brodie.* New York: Harper.

Spielberg, Steven, dir. 1998. *Saving Private Ryan.* Dreamworks. Film.

Spieler, Sophie. 2014. "Between Meritocracy and the Old Boy Network: Elite Education in Contemporary American Literature." *Current Objectives of Postgraduate American Studies* 10: 1–24.

Stapleton, Laurie. 2004. "Toward a New Learning: A Freirian Reading of Sapphire's *Push*." *Women Studies Quarterly* 32: 213–23.

Sternglass, Marilyn S. 1997. *Time to Know Them: A Longitudinal Study of Writing at the College Level.* New York: Routledge.

Stinson, John J. 2006, 2007. "Bennett's *The History Boys*: Unnoticed Ironies Lead to Critical Neglect." *Connotations* 16: 219–45.

Tierney, William G. 2002. "Interpreting Academic Identities: Reality and Fiction on Campus." *Journal of Higher Education* 73 (January): 161–72.

Tierney, William G. 2004. "Academic Freedom and Tenure: Between Fiction and Reality." *Journal of Higher Education* 75 (March): 161–77.

Traub, James. 1994. *City on a Hill: Testing the American Dream at City College.* New York: Da Capo.

Van Sant, Gus, dir. 2000. *Finding Forrester.* Columbia. Film.

Varnum, Robin. 1996. *Fencing with Words: A History of Writing Instruction at Amherst College during the Era of Theodore Baird, 1938–66.* Urbana, IL: National Council of Teachers of English.

von Sternberg, Josef, dir. 1930. *The Blue Angel.* Paramount. Film.

Waldman, Katy. 2018. "The New Yorker Recommends *Dear Committee Members*." *New Yorker* (May 21).

Weber, Bruce. 1992. "Mamet: Hearings Prompted *Oleanna*." *Chicago Tribune* (November 12). https://www.chicagotribune.com/news/ct-xpm-1992-11-12-9204120711-story.html.

Weir, Peter, dir. 1988. *Dead Poets Society.* Columbia. Film.

Willett, Jincy. 2008. *The Writing Class.* New York: St. Martin's.

Williams, Jeffrey J. 2012. "The Rise of the Academic Novel." *American Literary History* 24: 561–89.

Wineapple, Brenda. 2010. "Poetic Justice." *New York Times* (September 24).

Wolff, Melora. 2002. "The Writing Teacher on the Screen." *Chronicle of Higher Education* 48, no. 35 (May 10): B20.

Wolff, Tobias. 2004. *Old School.* New York: Knopf.

ABOUT THE AUTHOR

Joseph Harris is a professor of English at the University of Delaware, where he teaches composition and creative nonfiction. Previously, he directed the first-year writing programs at the University of Pittsburgh and Duke University. He has also served as editor of the *CCC* journal and the SWR book series. His other books from Utah State University Press are *Teaching with Student Texts, A Teaching Subject,* and *Rewriting: How to Do Things with Texts.*

INDEX